Just for Kicks
Oklahoma Route 66
Music Guide

by

George O. Carney
&
Hugh W. Foley, Jr.

NEW FORUMS PRESS INC.

Stillwater, Oklahoma, U.S.A. 2004

NEW FORUMS PRESS INC.

Published in the United States of America
by New Forums Press, Inc.
1018 S. Lewis St.
Stillwater, OK 74074
www.newforums.com

Library of Congress Cataloging-in-Publication Data

Carney, George O.
  Oklahoma Route 66 Music Guide / by George O. Carney &
Hugh W. Foley, Jr.
  ETC.

This book may be ordered in bulk quantities at discount from
New Forums Press, Inc., P.O. Box 876, Stillwater, OK 74076
[Federal I.D. No.]. Printed in the United States of America.

International Standard Book Number: 1-58107-090-X

Cover design by Mac Crank.

To Janie – The one I love
(GC)

To Nokose and Geri – My eternal traveling partners
(HF)

Contents

Foreword

This book would never have occurred to me had I not met George Carney in 1993. After studying with George, an Oklahoma State Regents Professor of Geography, while I was a graduate student at Oklahoma State University, we became good friends on our monthly rides from Muskogee to Stillwater where we served as board members of Friends of Oklahoma Music, the group responsible for inducting musicians with strong Oklahoma connections into the Oklahoma Music Hall of Fame.

Known as the "Dean of Music Geography"[1] by his colleagues, cohorts, and collaborators, George Carney (below) has made several important contributions to a field he has largely put on the map. His textbook, *The Sounds of People and Places*, now in its fourth edition, is *the* primary starting point for understanding how to contextualize music and musicians within the geographical area that produced those performers and the music they created. With the foundation of George's love for maps and what they can teach, our intense interest in preserving and promoting Oklahoma music history, and our collective music and data file collections, we began working on the *Oklahoma Music Guide* in 2002. Halfway through the production of that text, George had a stroke in December of 2003, from which he is still recovering, although he is able to still teach his popular classes at Oklahoma State. Much of his writing and research has fueled this book, however, and it is because of his biographical writings in the *Oklahoma Music Guide* that we were able to put together this guide to the musicians of Oklahoma's section of historic U.S. Route 66.

The first edition of the *Oklahoma Music Guide*, published in 2003, attempted to catalogue the major musicians, music groups, musical sounds, hit songs, and annual musical events that make Oklahoma a unique cultural environment that has produced major contributors to every form of American music. Beginning with the American Indian music of the 39 federally recognized tribes of Oklahoma, and continuing through the old time fiddle music of the first Anglo settlers, as well as the field hollers and spirituals brought by the slaves of African descent who accompanied their Southeastern tribal owners over the "Trail of Tears," one can hear the foundation of American popular music developing in the historic territories of the state. Follow up with the developing musical forms of ragtime, blues, country, singing cowboys, jazz, Western swing, honky tonk, R & B, and rock, and the evidence is clear that Oklahomans have made a startlingly impressive list of musical contributions to the world of music. Given the presence of the major population centers of Tulsa and Oklahoma City on Route 66, what's not so surprising is the number of Oklahoma musicians who also have significant connections to the highway whose own birth is linked directly to the 46th state.

About half of the musicians covered in the *Oklahoma Music Guide* have their roots, or an extremely strong connection, along the famous highway's path that itself has its beginnings in Tulsa via the vision of Cyrus Avery, a Tulsa businessman and Oklahoma's first highway commissioner, who led the national committee to create a national highway system in 1928. Subsequently, Avery advocated a Chicago-to-Los Angeles route that followed the earth's curvature south through Oklahoma. This is a well known story. However, of the myriad texts now available on Route 66, none pay any significant attention to the music of the Mother Road, other than a passing mention of someone famous, such as Garth Brooks, Roger Miller, or Patti Page, who were born in cities or towns along the highway in Oklahoma.Given the material we had already researched and written for the *Oklahoma Music Guide*, a smaller, more focused work on one branch of the Mother Text seemed like a logical idea. Also, this project offers us the opportunity to reprint a few essays from the first edition of the *Oklahoma Music Guide* with corrections, updating them based on feedback from our first run.

Another significant omission from any texts about Route 66 in Oklahoma is any explanation of the several American Indian tribes through whose historic and contemporary boundaries the road passes in Oklahoma. While this book makes no attempt to provide a complete history of these tribes and how they came to be where they are today, the *Oklahoma Route 66 Music Guide* does make a diligent effort to chronicle what is openly known about their musical traditions, and provide dates and locations of their annual events that are open to the public, usually free of charge. Safe to say, many Route 66 tourists who would enjoy seeing a powwow have no idea they are often passing right by one in the months between May and September.

This brings us to the other purposes for this guide. Too many times Route 66 is thought of as a relic of a past that has faded from the American landscape. Some of its dilapidated iconography is looked at with the same awe one feels when looking at dinosaur tracks. In the process of the highway's diminishing visibility,

the well-documented footprints left by the road are often the most sought-out elements by tourists and documentarians. However, modern Route 66 in Oklahoma unfurls through towns and cities that are often vibrant with commercial activity, cultural opportunities, and unique tourism spots found nowhere else in the world. There is no doubt that some Oklahoma small towns have suffered due to the interstate system bypassing their communities, but that same bypassing has also preserved quaint downtowns, fascinating historical structures, an abundance of enchanting countryside, and not just a few ghost stories.

For the music fan, Oklahoma is a treasure trove of American pop culture history, resplendent with towering musical personalities who have made major contributions to American Indian, blues, jazz, country, pop, new age, and classical music. Along Oklahoma's nearly 400 miles of Route 66, music enthusiasts can collect vintage albums for a fraction of their big-city prices, see and hear live music from one end of the state to the other, and buy reasonably priced musical instruments at any number of music stores and pawn shops. Would-be singers can try their own voice at numerous karaoke nights in bars and clubs across the state, or visit a number of museums and historic spots that flesh out the story of music in Oklahoma. This story is rapidly being understood as a microcosm of music in America: people from many different backgrounds living next door to each other, listening to each other play music, and creating their own dynamic sound that has ultimately taken its place on record players, juke boxes, radio stations, and now CD and MP3 players around the world. Of course a person should keep eyes peeled along Route 66 for the usual symbols that have come to represent the road in Oklahoma, but travelers should also keep ears open for the music of the old highway, past and present. After all, having some kicks is a big part of the trip.

Hugh Foley
Stillwater, Oklahoma
May, 2004

Endnote

1. While George Carney has made many significant contributions to the sub-field of music geography, he also points out that others led the way for him. Curt Sachs, in his *Meaning and Development of Musical Instruments* (1929), states there are "spatial aspects of music." In 1960, Paul Collaer developed *The Atlas Historique de la Musique*. Bruno Nettl mapped American Indian musical styles in 1954, and in 1964 Nettl authored *Theory in Ethnomusicology* in which he says, "Music must be studied in a spatial context." In 1960, Alan Lomax presented several maps in *Folk Songs of North America* and notes, "The map sings." Additionally, Norman Schafer launched The World Soundscape Project in 1971 that was followed by his *Music of the Environment* (1971) and *The Tuning of the World* (1977).

In the 1960s and 1970s, geographers began to study music. Lauren Post, one of Carl Sauer's students, included a chapter on music and dance in his *Cajun Sketches from the Prairies of Southwestern Louisiana* (1962). Peter H. Nash of the University of Waterloo published the first journal article on the subject with his "Music Regions and Regional Music" that appeared in *The Deccan Geographer*. Jeff Gordon completed the first master's thesis on music geography, "Rock and Roll: A Diffusion Study," in 1970 at Pennsylvania State University. The next year, a second master's thesis was completed by Ben Marsh, entitled "Sing Me Back Home: A Grammar of Places in Country Music Song," a portion of which was published by *Harper's Magazine* in 1977.

Also in the 1970s, the first scholarly article to appear in an American journal was Larry Ford's "Geographic Factors in the Origin, Evolution, and Diffusion of Rock and Roll," published by *The Journal of Geography* in 1971. In 1973, Larry and Tamara Stephenson authored an article entitled "A Prologue to

Listening" that appeared in *Antipode*. Also in 1973, Wilbur Zelinsky completed *The Cultural Geography of the United States* in which he writes that one of the untapped research topics for cultural geographers is music. And, finally, in 1978 Joseph Spencer, the distinguished cultural geographer at UCLA, wrote in "The Growth of the Cultural Geography," published in *The American Behavioral Scientist* that music is a fertile topic for cultural geographers to investigate.

Given this inspiration, George Carney began a torrent of scholarship on the subject of music geography. While a complete list of his publications is available through his Oklahoma State University website (www.geog.okstate.edu/staff/carney.htm), George's contributions to the field are as voluminous as they are broad. In 1990, he authored two scholarly articles: "Geography of Music: Inventory and Prospect" and "The Ozarks: A Reinterpretation Based on Folk Song Materials." In 1992, he compiled a monograph that is imperative reading for beginning Oklahoma music researchers: *Oklahoma Jazz Artists: A Biographical Dictionary*. In 1994, he published two more scholarly articles, "Branson: The New Mecca of Country Music" and "Oklahoma Jazz: Deep Second to 52nd Street," and published the 3rd edition of *The Sounds of People and Places: A Geography of American Folk and Popular Music*. George followed that up in 1995 with *Fast Food, Stock Cars, and Rock-n-Roll: Place and Space in American Pop Culture*. In 1996, *The Canadian Geographer* published his article "The Seven Themes of Music Geography," and the *Journal of Cultural Geography* published his essay, "Western North Carolina: Culture Hearth of Bluegrass Music." In 1998, Bowman and Littlefield published *Baseball, Barns, and Bluegrass: A Geography of American Folklife*, and the *Journal of Cultural Geography* published Carney's primary essay on the subject, "Music Geography."

In 1999, Carney continued his prolific output with "Cowabunga! Surfer Rock and the Five Themes of

Geography," and added "Western Swing in Fort Worth: Culture Hearth of the First Alternative Country Form" in 2000. With no letup in 2001, he published three more scholarly articles: "From Lee to Reba: Oklahoma Women in Popular Music," "Rockin' and Rappin' in American Music: Themes and Resources," and "American Music." The latter of those three was published in an Australian project, *America: The Complete Story*. In 2002, he contributed "Honky Tonk Angels and Rockabilly Queens: Oklahoma Divas in American Country Music" to the *Country Music Annual*, and exhibited his diverse interests and interpretive acumen in another essay, "Rappin' in the Midwest: Regionalization of a Music Genre." For most of the rest of 2002, George worked on the *Oklahoma Music Guide*, up until his stroke in December of that year. While he barely got to enjoy the release of the fourth edition of *The Sounds of People and Places: A Geography of American Music from Country to Classical and Blues to Bop* in 2003, he was able to use that text when he got back in the classroom during the summer of that year. Carney is back to teaching, with his ever-popular Geography of Music classes maxing out enrollment every semester, and he continues giving editorial advice on both the *Oklahoma Music Guide*, and keeping up with Oklahoma music via popular media and his service to the Oklahoma Music Hall of Fame Board of Directors. This guide to the music from Oklahoma's section of the Mother Road is an idea inspired by, and forever indebted to, George Carney's leadership in the fields of music geography and popular culture studies.

Just for Kicks: Oklahoma Route 66 Music Guide

Introduction

Traveling in from the east, Oklahoma is where U.S. Route 66 becomes exotic. Having crossed the Mississippi River, and rambled through the curves and hills of the Ozarks, the imaginations of tourists were tingled by historic images of Indian Country filled with frontier life on their way to the Grand Canyon and Disneyland. With Tulsa's art deco architecture and Oklahoma City's oil wells, however, those images had to be altered somewhat, but it was in between and on either side of those cities that gave old Route 66 its colorful status as a quirky, anything-is-possible journey where blue whales rise out of ponds in the east and giant kachinas bless the western sunset.

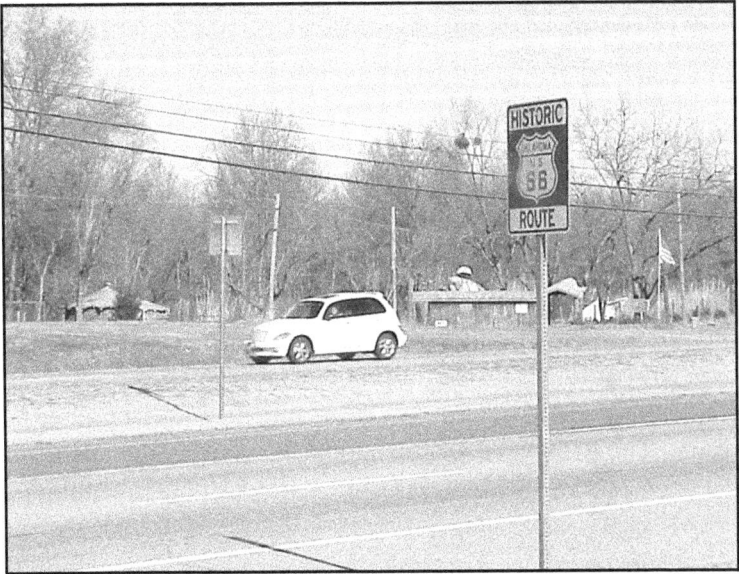

Topographically, Oklahoma's section of Route 66 is where the Ozark flint shelves of the northeastern part of the state gradually give way to rolling hills, red dirt, and, ultimately, the high plains. There, the West begins to unroll under the rubber, and the windshield becomes an extra-wide screen. Throughout the journey in Oklahoma, the multi-layered symbolism of Americana is at every turn: roadside signs indicating tribal nation borders; the rusty metal signs of advertising's yesteryear; crumbling and refurbished century-old buildings; Veterans of Foreign Wars clubs in most major towns, and some small ones; bridges now closed to anything not on foot; and friendly smiles cloaking the uncertainty of how one can make it through the off-season, when tourism slows to a trickle during the brown and gray Oklahoma winters.

Of course, as noted by several authors, the highway itself has become iconic. Its "yellow brick road" status as the Depression-era escape route for thousands of people in the 1930s branded those who traveled it to better themselves as an Okie, no matter if they were from Texas, Arkansas, or Kansas. While that term has been refurbished to imply those who pull themselves up from their bootstraps, some elder Oklahomans revile the term that is synonymous with anyone forced to leave Oklahoma, or other Great Plains areas, due to drought or destitution in the late 1930s.

John Steinbeck's *Grapes of Wrath* is routinely thought of as an essential depiction of the trip west. However, Steinbeck (right) puts the Joad family on their journey in east central Oklahoma, near Sallisaw, and the family does not join Route 66 until they get to Oklahoma City, some 150 miles to the west. The same is true for Woody Guthrie, whose "Talking Dust Bowl" is a hilarious and pointed account of the reasons for, and results of, leaving the Dust Bowl and heading for the West.[1] Woody's hometown of Okemah, however, was actually on U.S. 62, now I-40, and would have met old Route 66 in Oklahoma City about seventy miles west of Okemah. While Guthrie certainly sang about most every experience travelers had on the "Mother Road," a term Guthrie picked up from Steinbeck, it was two Pennsylvanians, Bobby and Cynthia

Troup, who forever mythologized the highway with their composition "Get Your Kicks on Route 66!" as recorded by Nat King Cole in 1946.[2] More so than any other pop cultural product, Troup's composition indicates the get-a-way highway as a place where people can have fun and forget about the job they have to get back to, or the school session that looms on the autumn horizon for kids bouncing around in the backseat.

A tremendous amount of music has been, and still is being, produced by the people who have, by happenstance or design, lived or worked along the famous thoroughfare. With the exception of the obvious music histories of Chicago and Los Angeles, Oklahomans have composed, written, conserved, or informally thought up an immense quantity American music, and often used the highway to take them to either of the larger cities on the end of the road. As chronicled by the authors in the *Oklahoma Music Guide*, musicians, groups, and tribal entities in the state have made significant contributions to every major genre of American music, and many of those musicians are directly connected to Oklahoma's stretch of U.S. Route 66.

Starting by looking at musicians in the extreme southwestern part of the state, Roger Miller ("King of the Road") and Sheb Wooley ("The Purple People Eater") both called Erick home. Jimmy Webb ("By the Time I Get to Phoenix") was born in Elk City, as was John Herren of the 1960s psychedelic outfit, The Electric Prunes. The #1 country music star in 2004, Toby Keith, was born in Clinton, along with one of Nashville's best-known contemporary producers, Scott Hendricks. Bob Wills' famous guitarist, Eldon Shamblin, was born in Weatherford, and free-jazz giant Sam Rivers is from El Reno. While Garth Brooks was born in Tulsa, he grew up in Yukon, and members of Cross Canadian Ragweed, perhaps the most successful of the red dirt artists on a national scale, are largely from Yukon and Calumet.

Oklahoma City can claim a multitude of significant musicians, as one would expect from the largest city in the state. Pop and rock groups such as Color Me Badd and the Flaming Lips have their origins in the capitol city, as do jazz men Jimmy Rushing, Don Cherry, Wardell Gray, and Benny Garcia, Jr. Although born in Texas, *the* primary jazz guitarist, Charlie Christian, was reared in Oklahoma City and had his first musical experiences there before joining the Benny Goodman Orchestra. Country music has enjoyed the contributions of OKC natives such Alvin Crow, Henson Cargill, Wiley and Gene, Tyler England, Tommy Overstreet, Greg Jennings of Restless Heart, and the Red Dirt Rangers' John Cooper, as well as providing Conway Twitty with his base of operations for much of the 1960s. Rockers who came out of Oklahoma City included J.J. Cale (even though he moved to Tulsa as a youngster), all-world bassist Carl Radle, Barry "Eve of Destruction" McGuire, and 1950s rockabilly artist Tommy Collins.

Moving up north and east on 66 through Edmond, travelers can treat themselves to live music at the UCO jazz lab (at right), just a couple of blocks off the historic path, and then make their way to Arcadia, birthplace of noted jazz bandleader, Al Dennie.

Next, Wellston is the birthplace of country songstress Norma Jean, and Chandler is the town where adventurous classical composer Roy Harris was born before his parents got on the "paradise highway" and left for California. Thanks to Leota and John Gillian, who did not leave town, sons Steve and Russell Gillian have been National Grand Champion Fiddle and Guitar players, respectively.

Bristow is home to Grammy-nominated folksinger Tom Paxton, and is also home to the Skinner Brothers, Tom, Mike and Craig, all of whom made early and continuing contributions to the hybrid musical form known as Red Dirt Music, a loose term for several musicians who moved in and out of the college town of Stillwater, all the while playing music that is a combination of blues, country, rock and roll, Tin Pan Alley, cowboy songs, and folk music. Skinner has co-written perhaps the most poignant song by an Oklahoman about Route 66, "Used to Be." Just northeast of Bristow, Sapulpa celebrates Marshal Royal, the lead alto and sax player for the Count Basie Orchestra for almost twenty years (1951 – 1970), with an annual jazz festival in his honor over the first weekend of June.

Tulsa is also extremely rich with music history and significant musicians, some of whom were born there, and some of whom moved there. The latter includes Bob Wills and his brothers Luke, Johnnie Lee, and Billy Jack (pictured at right in that order with Bob in the white scarf), J.J. Cale, Leon Russell, Jack Dunham, Elvin Bishop, Ronnie Dunn of Brooks

& Dunn, and members of Jacob Fred Jazz Odyssey. A partial list of native Tulsa musicians who have made a strong impact on the national scene run the gamut of styles and eras: Tuck Andress (new age guitarist); Garth Brooks, Gus Hardin, and Joe Diffie (country); David Gates, Dwight Twilley, and Hanson (pop); Wayman Tisdale, Earl Bostic, Cecil McBee, and Howard McGhee (jazz); The GAP Band and Toni Estes (R & B).

Moving northeast out of Tulsa picks up the musical strains of Claremore natives Patti Page and all-everything session drummer Jim Keltner, as well as dramatist Lynn Riggs, whose play *Green Grow the Lilacs* formed the basis for the musical *Oklahoma!* Miami's musical stars are linked to the Southern rock movement of the 1970s with Cassie and Steve Gaines who were members of Lynyrd Skynyrd at the time of that group's tragic plane crash in which both young musicians were killed. Finally, Quapaw produced one of the 20th century's most significant classical musicians from Oklahoma, Louis Ballard, whose Quapaw and Cherokee ancestry illuminate the often-overlooked musical and historic element of Route 66 in Oklahoma, the eleven tribal nations through which the road passes.

Following tribal boundaries and knowing what is Indian Country and what is not is very tricky. The reason is because of the 19th century allotment process that carved up tribal lands for American Indians, and opened up the rest for non-Indian settlement. As a result of that and many unscrupulous land grabs, Indian Country in Oklahoma might best be described as a checkerboard, with some here and some there. However, the borders of tribal lands that were established in treaties up through the 1870s still stand. Alert travelers may notice tribal license plates on many cars in Oklahoma, and they are most prominent in the areas still considered Indian Country. Not including the history of the tribes such as the Osage, Pawnee, Kiowa, and Comanche, for whom much of Oklahoma was a hunting ground prior to the arrival of the Europeans, Route 66 travelers pass through eleven tribal jurisdictions in Oklahoma (Map 3), and that does not include tribes such as the Modoc and Miami, whose tribal offices are in Miami, nor the Seneca-Cayuga, Wyandotte (known in history as the Hurons), and the Eastern Shawnee, whose lands and headquarters are very close by. Entering from the northeast, travelers go through lands that once belonged to tribes removed to Indian Territory in the 19th century, to include in order from east to west: Quapaw, Peoria, Ottawa, Cherokee, Muscogee (Creek), Sac and Fox, Kickapoo, Cheyenne and Arapaho, and finally the Wichita, Caddo, Delaware joint reservation, before crossing back into Cheyenne and Arapaho country. A turn north on Highway 177 at Warwick puts one into the Iowa Tribe of Oklahoma's land about 1/10th of a mile from Route 66. As a result, we have included the Iowa Tribe, significant musicians from the tribe, and their annual powwow in the guide.

Oklahoma possesses a rich and variegated musical heritage and music that has proven to be one of its most important cultural resources. Along with many of the major musical names mentioned in this essay, the state has spawned influential institutions, including ballrooms such as Cain's, near Route 66 in Tulsa, and the Diamond in Oklahoma City; radio stations like KVOO in Tulsa and WKY in Oklahoma City; and nurtured bands such as the Texas Playboys and the Oklahoma City Blue Devils. It has also produced some of the most respected producers in the music industry, including Lucky Moeller, Tim Dubois, and Scott Hendricks. Noted instrumentalists, such as Eldon Shamblin, Barney Kessel, Oscar Pettiford, and Jesse Ed Davis, were born in Oklahoma. Finally, songs such as "Oklahoma!," "Oklahoma Hills," "You're the Reason God Made Oklahoma," "Okie From Muskogee," and "Take Me Back to Tulsa," not only evoke images of Oklahoma, but are a significant part of the American music legacy.

The question remains, however, why Oklahoma is such a fertile ground for the production of music artists, composers, and institutions when compared with other states?

One must first consider the settlement patterns of Oklahoma because they reflect the cultural diversity of the state. Charles N. Gould, an early twentieth century travel writer and geographer, emphasizes Oklahoma's multicultural traditions: "Oklahoma is a meeting place of many different peoples. Nowhere else is there such a mingling of types. Practically every state in the Union and every civilized nation on the globe is represented among the state's inhabitants."[3] Many different cultural groups brought music in their "cultural baggage" resulting in the development of a myriad of vibrant musical subcultures. This vast array of people and their music includes the songs and dance music of the American Indian from the southeastern United States and western plains, northeastern woodlands, Great Lakes, and Ohio Valley; Anglo-Celtic ballads from the upland South; country blues from the Mississippi

Delta; black and white spirituals from the lowland South; European immigrant music from Italy, Germany, and Czechoslovakia; polka music from the upper Midwest; and Mexican *mariachi* from the Rio Grande Valley. This musical mixture is further reflected in the *WPA Guide to 1930s Oklahoma*: "each successive immigrant to the state brought the dust of another locale on his feet and the lilt of another people's song on his lips."[4]

This cultural confluence of different genres of American music allowed Oklahomans to experiment, innovate, and improvise—traits necessary in the formulation of various forms of American music. Within this Oklahoma cultural mosaic, music knew no color. Black, white, and red musicians borrowed freely from each other, exchanged repertoires and musical ideas, and adopted new techniques and styles. These cross-cultural experiences favored the development of music in Oklahoma. Noted folklorist Alan Lomax's statement that "the map sings"[5] is a fitting description for the music of Oklahoma.

A second factor is Oklahoma's population characteristics and economic history. The diversity of indigenous musical influences provides the state with roots and foundations of the twentieth century powwow world, with home-grown groups, such as Thunderhorse, Bad Moon Rising, Young Bird, Yellow Hammer, Southern Thunder, Poor Boys, and Grayhorse, as well as a cornucopia of tribal ceremonial musics. From the Kiowa Gourd Dance songs and Caddo Turkey Dance songs, to Ponca war dance songs, Cheyenne-Arapaho Sun Dance songs, Wichita Friendship songs, and Pawnee hand game songs, Oklahoma's indigenous music is deep and ancient.

Furthering the unique story of the tribes in Oklahoma is the connection between the Southeastern tribes and the slaves of African descent who were removed with the tribes, beginning in the 1820s. As the Cherokee, Choctaw, Muscogee (Creek), Seminole, and Chickasaw were forced to migrate to Indian Territory beginning in the 1820s, several tribal members brought slaves who endured the same "Trail of Tears" as the owners they accompanied. Thus, a plantation culture emerged in Oklahoma in which the spirituals, work songs, and blues of the African-American developed much as they did in other parts of the rural South.

For example, three African-American spirituals are believed to have been composed in the 1840s by "Uncle" Wallace and "Aunt" Minerva Willis, slaves on a large plantation near Doaksville in the Choctaw Nation. The authenticity and origin of spirituals are seldom credited to individuals; however, field researchers noted that the Willis family sang "Swing Low, Sweet Chariot," "Steal Away to Jesus," and "I'm a Rollin'" in the cotton fields of Reverend Alexander Reid, superintendent of a Choctaw boarding school. Reid wrote the words and music and forwarded the transcriptions to the Jubilee Singers at Fisk University in Nashville. Subsequently, the group sang the numbers on a tour of the United States and Europe.[6]

Evolving from the Oklahoma African-American work songs and spirituals, with additional musical developments due to the connection between slave-holding Southeastern tribes, the country blues established itself in Indian Territory and Oklahoma via the same plantation and sharecropping milieu that existed in the South. The first-known, commercially-printed blues in music history, "Dallas Blues," was published by Oklahoma City's Hart Wand in 1912, three months before W.C. Handy's "Memphis Blues," which is generally thought of, however inaccurately, as the first published blues. Additionally, because of the large African-American population in the state, significant musicians such as ragtime pianist Scott Joplin are known to have played in the Indian Territory, and the great Mississippi blues man Robert Johnson played in the all-black town of Taft. Traveling territory bands, such as the Oklahoma City Blue Devils, brought the hot swinging music of the Southwest to black audiences in Oklahoma, Kansas, and Missouri. While the style of music may have found its summit in

Kansas City, many primary musicians came from Oklahoma, such as Jimmy Rushing, "Buddy" Anderson, and saxophonist Don Byas, just a fraction of the jazz musicians from the state. Popular rhythm and blues eventually flourished in the personages of such noted Oklahoma-born blues artists as Jay McShann, Lowell Fulson, Robert Jeffrey, Roy Milton, and Joe Liggins, not to mention the "father of funk guitar," Jimmy Nolen, who made his fame as James Brown's primary guitarist on hits such as "Papa's Got a Brand New Bag" and "I Got You (I Feel Good)."

Alongside the American Indian and African-American music traditions, the oldest Anglo-American music forms migrated into the state when tribal lands opened for settlement with the five land runs beginning in 1889. With this additional layer of music came the fiddle dance tunes, such as the reels, hornpipes, jigs, schottisches, and strathspeys,[7] while other Oklahomans worshipped to the melodies of Old Time and Southern Gospel music. Albert E. Brumley, born in rural LeFlore County, composed three of the best-known gospel songs in American music history: "I'll Fly Away," "Turn Your Radio On," and "Jesus Hold My Hand." Significant contemporary contributors to Christian music who have roots in the state include Susie Luchsinger, Sandy Patti, and Point of Grace.

Oklahoma's population is small town and rural-oriented, both in terms of composition and aesthetics. Moreover, the rural and small town residents have experienced considerable poverty throughout the state's history. Both the rural nature of the state and the poverty challenges confronted by its residents favored the development of various genres of American music, particularly country. Oklahoma's high percentage of tenant farmers and sharecroppers in the past forced many to seek music as an avenue for leaving poverty. Several musicians were children of Great Depression parents who had survived the hard times and dust—parents who longed for a better life for their family, such as Merle Haggard, Chet Baker, Bonnie Owens, and Jean Shepard. Subsequently, the parents encouraged their sons and daughters to practice their musical talents and promoted them at any venue available within Oklahoma. A number of Oklahoma-based musicians helped turn music into a profession, including Otto Gray and the Oklahoma Cowboys, Gene Autry, Bob Wills, and Hank Thompson.

Many young children in Oklahoma's rural areas and small towns sought a more secure economic lifestyle. When they listened to the radio broadcasts of Otto Gray over KFRU (Bristow), Johnny Bond on WKY (Oklahoma City), and Gene Autry and Bob Wills on KVOO (Tulsa) during the first half of the twentieth century, it helped inspire them to become professional musicians. Virtually every sub-genre of country music can attribute substantial elements of its growth to Oklahomans or musicians commonly associated with Oklahoma, including singing cowboys (Gene Autry), cowboy bands (Otto Gray), Western swing (Spade Cooley and Bob Wills), honky tonk (Willis Brothers), country pop (Roger Miller), progressive or "outlaw" (Ray Wylie Hubbard), "Bakersfield Sound" (Tommy Collins and Bonnie Owens), "Nashville Sound" (Vince Gill, Reba McEntire, and Ronnie Dunn), and alternative country (Cross Canadian Ragweed and The Great Divide). As a result, the Anglo-American tradition of country music may be the most recognized musical export from the state, validated by Country Music Television's 2003 list of the "40 Greatest Men of Country Music," a list that includes ten names, or 25% of that group, are strongly associated with Oklahoma. Four of the men were born in the state (Toby Keith, Garth Brooks, Vince Gill, and Roger Miller). Gene Autry moved to Oklahoma as an infant, Merle Haggard was born to Okie migrants who left during the Great Depression, and the other four (Bob Wills, Buck Owens, Conway Twitty, and Ronnie Dunn) came to Oklahoma for extended performance opportunities. Native-born Oklahoma women who made the

2003 CMT "Top 40 Women of Country Music" include Reba McEntire and Wanda Jackson.

As a neutral gauge of Oklahoma's impact on country music, the 2003 CMT "100 Greatest Songs of Country Music" included nineteen songs with connections to the state. Included in the top ten are Merle Kilgore's "Ring of Fire" (#4); Garth Brooks' performance of "Friends in Low Places" (#6); "Galveston" (#8), written by Jimmy Webb; and "Behind Closed Doors" (#9), written by Kenny O'Dell. Other songs with Oklahoma connections making the list include Garth Brooks' "The Dance" (#14), Conway Twitty's "Hello Darlin'" (#17), Merle Haggard's "Okie From Muskogee" (#21), Reba McEntire's "Fancy" (#27), Roger Miller's "King of the Road" (#37), Vince Gill's "When I Call Your Name" (#44), Brooks and Dunn's "Boot Scootin' Boogie" (#48), Vince Gills' "Go Rest High on That Mountain" (#60), Patti Page's "Tennessee Waltz" (#63), Reba McEntire's "Is There Life Out There?" (#79), Toby Keith's "Should've Been a Cowboy" (#82), Gene Autry's "Have I Told You Lately That I Love You" (#88), Bob Wills' "Faded Love" (#98), and Gene Autry's "Back in the Saddle Again" (#99). And that does not even include "Take Me Home Country Roads" (#18) by John Denver who spent his teen summers on his grandfather's wheat farm in Bessie, Oklahoma. Therefore, almost one fifth of the 100 greatest songs of country music, according to CMT, have connections to Oklahoma.

A third factor in Oklahoma's historic music growth focuses on the availability of performance venues. As these young Oklahoma musicians honed their musical skills at county fairs, churches, school assemblies, nightclubs, and music contests and festivals throughout the state, many eventually found the opportunity to perform on the state's live music radio shows, such as KLPR in Oklahoma City and KTUL in Tulsa. Moreover, public dance halls and ballrooms, virtually nonexistent before the 1920s, proliferated in great numbers to accommodate the new wave of dance styles, e.g., fox trot, sweeping the country. The Ritz and Trianon Ballrooms in Oklahoma City, Casa Loma and Louvre Ballrooms in Tulsa, and the Bluebird Ballroom in Shawnee provided important outlets for amateur musicians to perform for these dances. Finally, Oklahoma music festivals, such as Grant's Old Time Country and Bluegrass Festival in Hugo, the oldest festival of its type west of the Mississippi, showcased such budding artists as Vince Gill, Joe Diffie, and Jimmy Henley. As a result, these local experiences helped Oklahomans launch their professional careers in music and simultaneously inspired younger musicians in Oklahoma to seek music as a profession.

A fourth and final factor in the state's vast musical output is the numerous local musicians who were influential in the early development of many musical careers. Music teachers, such as Zelia N. Page Breaux, Evelyn Sheffield, and Cornelius Pittman at Douglass High School in Oklahoma City; Ashley Alexander at Edison High School in Tulsa; George Bright at Sapulpa High School; and the Manual Training High School in Muskogee provided sound formal training for aspiring jazz musicians. Local Oklahoma bandleaders, such as Ernie Fields, Eddie Christian, Merl Lindsay, and Hank Thompson, offered opportunities, such as singing or playing instruments in bands and performing on live radio shows, and assisted hopeful musicians in securing recording contracts.

Music is one of the cultural traits that make Oklahoma a unique place, distinguishing the state from other places and giving special meaning to its residents—a feeling of pride in place. Psychologists call it "shared ego," while cultural geographers refer to it as "place consciousness." Place itself embodies meaning dependent upon the personal history that one brings to it. It is through these people-place interactions that one develops a deep psychological attachment with a specific place, such as Oklahoma.

Recognition and appreciation of the contributions and innovations of Oklahomans in American music can help create a sense of local awareness and, translated correctly, can become a source of state pride. The Oklahoma Jazz Hall of Fame in Tulsa and the Oklahoma Music Hall of Fame in Muskogee are positive steps in this direction.

Oklahomans are awakening to a seemingly neglected segment of the state's cultural history and are now paying tribute to those who participated in its development. When the names of Jimmy Rushing, Lowell Fulson, Nokie Edwards, Wanda Jackson, or Jesse Ed Davis are mentioned to Oklahomans, few know the significance of these musicians to American music or even realize they are Oklahomans. By contrast, political, religious, and sports figures native to Oklahoma, such as Carl Albert, Oral Roberts, and Mickey Mantle, are easily recognized. Therefore, cultural historians, educators, and state arts organizations have a responsibility to teach the citizens of the state the multifaceted aspects of their culture, including the role Oklahomans have played in American music.

Twentieth century popular music from Oklahoma is just another example of the state's significant contributions to the national music scene. Among the notable pop composers are Elk City's Jimmy Webb ("Up, Up and Away," "By the Time I Get to Phoenix," "Galveston," "Wichita Lineman," and "MacArthur Park") and Duncan's Hoyt Axton ("Joy to the World," "Greenback Dollar," "The Pusher," and "Boney Fingers"). Known musicians who have landed in the pop mainstream since the 1960s include a host of Tulsa Sound veterans: David Gates, Leon Russell, J.J. Cale, Elvin Bishop, and The GAP Band. Late twentieth century #1 pop successes include Color Me Badd and Hanson, and the critically acclaimed Flaming Lips, who won a GRAMMY award in 2003 for Best Instrumental Rock Song. Several groups and individuals with Oklahoma foundations, such as Admiral Twin, Ultrafix, Caroline's Spine, Toni Estes, Tony Romanello, Kings of Leon, and the All-American Rejects, are gainingnational stature in the pop *milieu*, Additionally, the roster of red dirt music artists from Oklahoma includes its elders, Bob Childers, Tom Skinner, and Jimmy LaFave; its workhorse ambassadors,

The Red Dirt Rangers; and its young guns, Jason Boland, Stoney LaRue, and Amanda Cunningham. While one red dirt band, The Great Divide, rode the major label train and decided to get off, Cross Canadian Ragweed (at right), with previously mentioned roots in Yukon and Calumet, had its

major label ticket punched in 2001 and has enjoyed national video and radio airplay, international distribution, and a rabid following regionally and nationally. Their 2004 release, *Soul Gravy* (Universal South), entered the country album charts at #5 on after its release in March of that year.

Musicologists agree that music is one of the most important indicators of the cultural *milieu* of an area. With the culture of Oklahoma facing increased homogeneity, music remains an enduring characteristic of its changing lifestyle. Historically, Oklahomans have always reacted against cultural conformity. Perhaps the rebellious attitude of a youthful state encourages this demeanor; the unique mixture of the people who settled here may also explain such an ethos. Music is a direct form of expression. One can examine in depth the role of Oklahomans in music—their way of life, value systems, aspirations, and misery. Thus, music is a key to understanding the cultural history of the state. As H. Wayne and Anne Hodges Morgan write in the state's bicentennial history:

A sense of the past delineates the shape of things to come, since all change is rooted in history. It also reveals tasks that must be fulfilled to secure the state's proper future. A general desire for cultural activities is the state's greatest present lack and future need. . . .Oklahoma must emphasize her native cultural qualities and encourage outlets for cultural ambition designed from national models. Oklahoma's economy is no longer provincial; her culture cannot remain so.[8]

Oklahoma's performers, composers, music institutions, and songs are a significant part of the rich and diversified musical heritage of the state, but, more importantly, this state-based perspective provides us with a fuller and deeper appreciation of the American music landscape. As the scholarship associated with American music continues to increase, so does the need for more in-depth research into regional studies of music. When completed, fuller documentation of music at the state level will become a vital component of American music history.[9] We hope the *Oklahoma Music Guide* series and its accompanying documentation will encourage students, teachers, fans, and scholars to continue appreciating, researching, and writing about the great array of Oklahoma music and its contributions to world culture. With the *Oklahoma Route 66 Music Guide* specifically, we hope to encourage a new brand of cultural adventure - musical tourism. Our goals include sharing the state's profound musical legacy; providing those interested with a beacon for finding its current musical activities and sites of interest; documenting the players and singers of Oklahoma's stretch of Route 66 who have made music history; and, of course, keeping our ears open for whatever is going to happen next.

George Carney and Hugh Foley
May, 2004,
Stillwater, Oklahoma

Endnotes

1. For more of Woody Guthrie's personal perspective on the Dust Bowl, Okies, the Mother Road, et al., refer to his spoken commentary on *Woody Guthrie: Library of Congress Recordings*. Cambridge, Mass.: Rounder CD 1041-1043, 1989.

2. For an extensive discussion of the origins, development, and ultimate significance of "Get Your Kicks on Route 66," see Arthur Krim's essay, "Get Your Kick on Route 66!" in *The Sounds of People and Places* (4th edition), George O. Carney, editor (Lanham, MD: Rowman and Littlefield, 2003), 137-48.

3. Charles N. Gould. *Travels Through Oklahoma* (Oklahoma City: Harlow Publishing Company, 1928), 157. See also Michael Frank Doran, "The Origins of Culture Areas in Oklahoma, 1893-1900," Unpublished Ph.D. dissertation, Department of Geography, University of Oregon, 1974, and Michael Roark, "Searching for the Hearth: Culture Areas of Oklahoma," *The Chronicles of Oklahoma* 70 (Winter 1992-93), 416-31.

4. Writers' Program of the Works Progress Administration. 1986. *The WPA Guide to 1930s Oklahoma*. (Lawrence: University Press of Kansas, rev. ed.), 104.

5. Alan Lomax. 1960. *The Folks Songs of North America* (Garden City, NY: Doubleday), xv.

6. *The WPA Guide to 1930s Oklahoma*, 105-06.

7. James Hubert Renner. 1974. "Geographic Implications of the Fiddling Tradition in Oklahoma," Unpublished Master's thesis, Department of Geography, Oklahoma State University.

8. H. Wayne Morgan and Anne Hodges Morgan. 1977. *Oklahoma: A Bicentennial History* (New York: W. W. Norton), 176.

9. Along these lines, Burton W. Peretti in his review essay "The Jazz Studies Renaissance" has called for more regional studies of jazz. See Burton W. Peretti. "The Jazz Studies Renaissance," *American Studies* 34 (1993), 139-49.

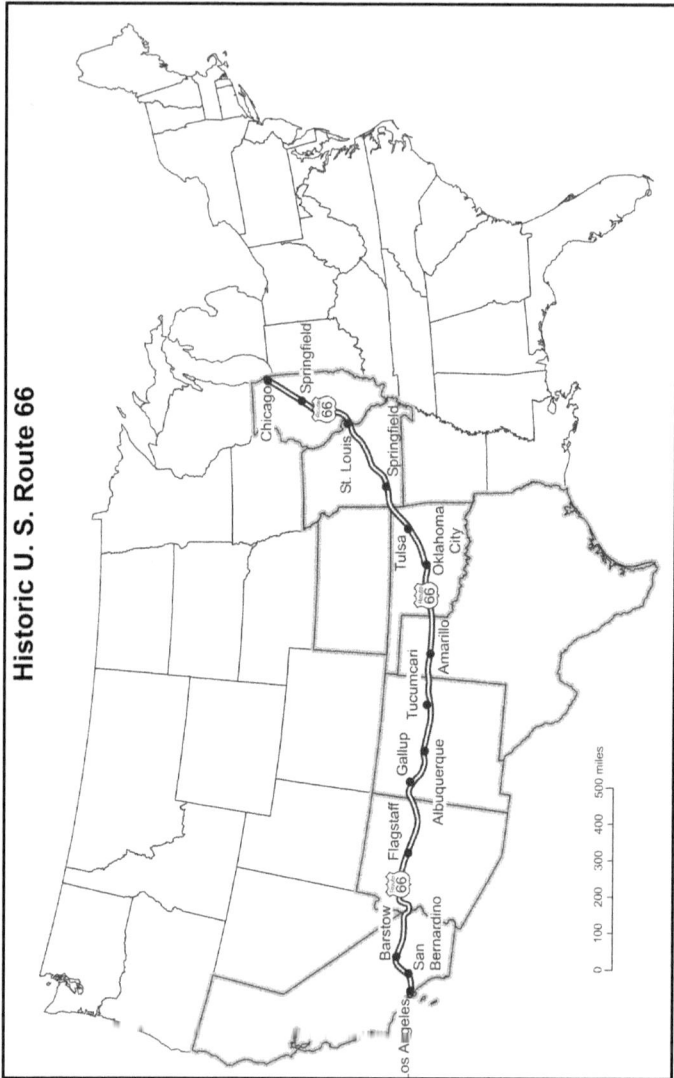

Map 1: Historic U.S. Route 66

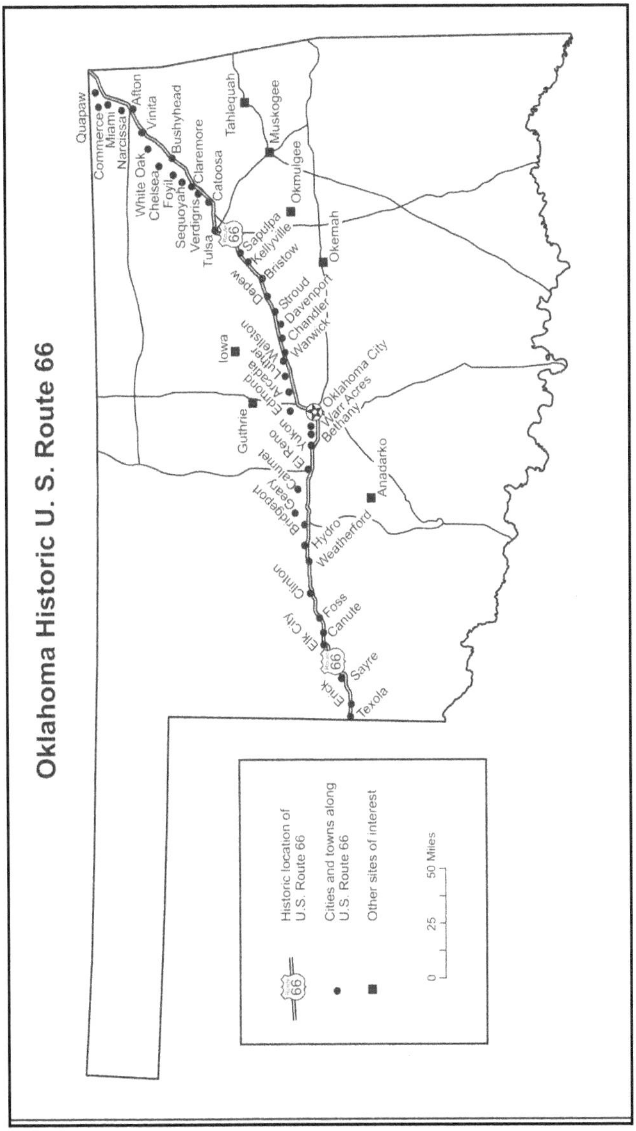

Map 2: Oklahoma Historic U.S. Route 66

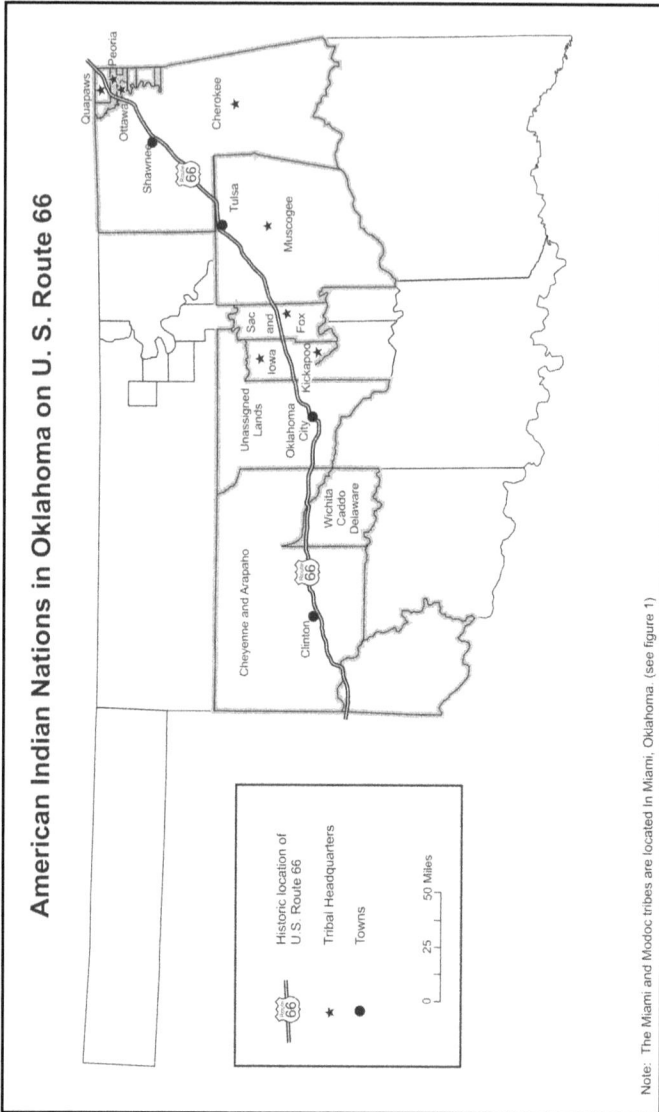

American Indian Nations in Oklahoma on U. S. Route 66

Historic location of U.S. Route 66

Tribal Headquarters

Towns

0   25   50 Miles

Note: The Miami and Modoc tribes are located in Miami, Oklahoma. (see figure 1)

Map 3. American Indian nations on Route 66. Additional nations are outlined but not named. While the Modoc's tribal allotment area is the small square in the northeastern corner of the state, the tribe's offices are in Miami. Additionally, the Miami Tribe's land is joined with the Ottawa's land, which is why there is not a specific national outline for the Miami.

Oklahoma Route 66 Music Guide

From East to West

When arriving in Oklahoma from the east on Route 66,

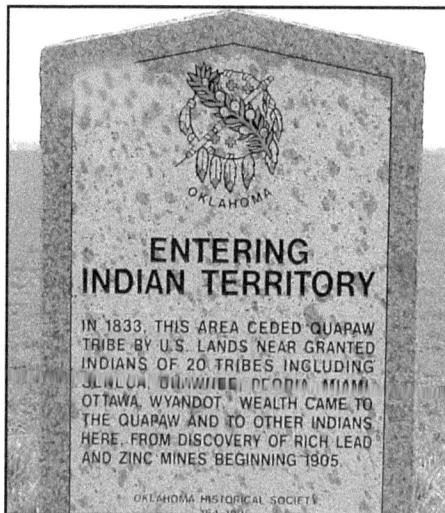

ENTERING
INDIAN TERRITORY

IN 1833, THIS AREA CEDED QUAPAW
TRIBE BY U.S. LANDS NEAR GRANTED
INDIANS OF 20 TRIBES INCLUDING
SENECA, SHAWNEE, PEORIA, MIAMI,
OTTAWA, WYANDOT. WEALTH CAME TO
THE QUAPAW AND TO OTHER INDIANS
HERE, FROM DISCOVERY OF RICH LEAD
AND ZINC MINES BEGINNING 1905.

OKLAHOMA HISTORICAL SOCIETY

travelers are officially in Indian Territory.

Quapaw

Year Established: 1897
2000 Population: 984

History Brief

Named after the nearby Quapaw Tribe, the town's coexistence with the area's lead and zinc history has resulted in the controversial greyish hills around the area known as "chat" piles, as well as critical environmental and health challenges for the people of the area. The issue received national coverage in the April 26, 2004, issue of *Time* magazine.

Annual Music Event

Quapaw Powwow, July 2, 3, 4th. Public welcome.
Beaver Springs Park, Quapaw Tribal Headquarters,
2.5 Miles East of Quapaw, on Future Farmer Road.

Notable Area Musicians

Wayne Walker   Country Songwriter
Born: December 13, 1927, in Quapaw
Died: January 2, 1979, in Nashville, Tennessee
Notable Music: Walker co-wrote the 1957 hit, "I've Got a New Heartache" with Ray Price, and also became widely known for songs such as "Are You Sincere," recorded by Elvis Presley, and for which Walker won a BMI Million Airplay Award.

Rascal Flatts: Gary LeVox, Joe Don Rooney, and Jay De Marcus

Joe Don Rooney   Guitarist, vocalist for Rascal Flatts
Born: September 13, 1975 in Baxter Springs, Kansas. Raised in Picher, attended Picher-Cardin High School.
Notable Music: Platinum albums *Rascal Flatts* (2000) and *I Melt* (2002) earned the group several top vocal group awards from the Country Music Association, Academy of Country Music, and Country Music Television.

Jimmmie Rivers
Western swing Bandleader,
Guitarist

Born: 1926 in Hockerville
Notable Music: For the best
examples of Rivers' "country-
jazz," seek out Jimmie Rivers
and the Cherokees featuring
Vance Terry, *Brisbane Bop:
Western Swing 1961-64*
(Joaquin Records, 1995).

For More Information About Quapaw
Quapaw City Hall (918) 674-2525

Quapaw Tribe of Oklahoma

The ancient roots of the
Quapaw Tribe of Okla-
homa lie in a group of
Sioux-speaking people
known as the Dhegiha
(pronounced "Day-gee-ha),
or "people on our side," a
large body which split into
the tribes known today as
the Quapaw, Osage,
Ponca, Kansa, and Omaha.
After the split of the main
group the Quapaw became known by their Dhegiha relatives
as the "downstream people," with their name pronounced,
roughly, "Oh-gahf-pah."

The Quapaw stayed in villages along the Arkansas River not far from its mouth until Europeans and American settlers began pushing them out. By 1818, the Quapaw began ceding land to the United States to insure the tribe's well-being, but that well-being never really took place as the tribe relocated several times before stabilizing in 1852 on their reservation in Indian Territory.

Located between the Grand River and the Missouri state line in what is now northeastern Ottawa County, the Quapaw Reservation was overrun during the Civil War by both sides, and tribal members had to remove themselves to Kansas and wait out the conflict. Upon returning, the people slowly rebuilt their homes and nation, endured the 1890s' allotment process in which the reservation was parceled out to tribal members, and, finally, in 1905 the tribe learned massive amounts of zinc and lead deposits were buried underneath tribal lands.

The discovery of minerals first proved fruitful for tribal members, but at the end of the twentieth century had created one of the nation's largest and oldest federal Superfund cleanup sites. While adults have no trouble resisting the lead, under no circumstances should travelers with small children explore the interesting looking, but certainly hazardous, mounds of "chat" that surround Quapaw and Commerce. The subject is a source of much local discontent, discussion and political wrangling. Currently, the tribal headquarters near Quapaw is also the site of the annual Quapaw powwow, which celebrated its 132nd anniversary in 2004. Free and open to the public, it features intertribal dancing and contests, as well as specialty dances such as the Chicken Dance and Lady's Fancy Dance.

Notable Musical Traditions and Musicians

George Valliere, third from left, joins in with with some of Oklahoma's finest powwow singers.

While some tribal members participate in the Native American Church where the peyote songs are sung, the majority of Quapaw musical traditions have been absorbed by the intertribal powwow world. The best-known Quapaw contemporary powwow singer is George Valliere, Jr., who is also Shawnee. He has recorded with the intertribal singing group Southern Thunder for Indian House Records, and is also a regular head singer as powwows across Oklahoma.

Louis Ballard   Educator, Classical Composer
Born: July 8, 1931, on Devil's Promenade, near Quapaw
Notability: A wide-ranging composer who has written many types of music for all instruments and voices, Louis W. Ballard's Quapaw name, Honganózhe, means "Grand Eagle."
   Ballard's credits include music premiers at Lincoln Center New York, John F. Kennedy Center in Washington D.C., the Smithsonian Institution, Carnegie Hall, the Hollywood Bowl and other major venues around the world.

Louis Ballard (right) has been awarded grants from the Rockefeller Foundation, Ford Foundation, and National Endowment for the Arts, and, in 1989, he was the first American composer to present an entire program of his music in the Beethoven-House Chamber Music Hall adjoining Beethoven's birthplace. In 1997, Ballard was presented a Lifetime Achievement Award from the First Americans in the Arts, and The Oklahoma Music Hall of Fame in Muskogee inducted Louis Ballard its 2004 class.

In 1974, Ballard composed *Incident at Wounded Knee* (1974). The piece memorialized the tragedies of the Oglala Sioux in 1890 at Wounded Knee, South Dakota, and resonated with the American Indian Movement's conflict with the U.S. government at Wounded Knee in 1973. While he believes in the piece as rooted in history, Ballard has written he hoped it would "rise above all political emotions of this epoch."

Commerce

Established: 1913
2000 Population: 2,645

Like Quapaw and Miami, Commerce was also a mining town, but is best-known for producing New York Yankees baseball legend Mickey Mantle. Mantle was actually born in Spavinaw, about thirty-five miles southwest of Commerce, but moved here only a few years later to a humble home at 319 S. Quincy, which still stands today and is open to visitors. Call (918) 542-6087 for more information.

For Vinyl Collectors

For one of the best collections of used vinyl in the area, visit the Commerce Flea Market at 113 Commerce St. Business hours are Monday through Saturday, 10 a.m. to 6 p.m., Sunday, 11 a.m. to 2 p.m.

Music Venues

Hattie's Club on Commerce Street since November 1, 1949.

For More Information

Commerce City Hall
(918) 675-4373

Peoria Tribe of Oklahoma

Brief Tribal History

Beginning their known historical origins at the mouth of Wisconsin River near Prairie du Chien, Wisconsin, bands of the tribe began moving south in the 1600s to the area near present-day Peoria, Illinois. Some Peoria people who survived the French and Indian War allied themselves with the Wea Tribe on the Blackwater Fork of the Illinois River near St. Genevieve, Missouri, but the main group stayed on the Illinois. By treaties with the United States in 1818 and 1832, the remaining people of the Illinois Confederacy were united with the Peoria, to include the Kaskaskia and Piankashaw, and the entire group moved to present-day Miami County, Kansas, under the moniker of the Confederate Peoria.

Harassed and duped by settlers, Kansas state law, and illegal taxation on their property, many of the people lost their lands in Kansas. After the Civil War, the government proceeded with its strategy to remove all tribes from Kansas to Indian Territory. The Confederated Peoria relocated to Indian Territory to a tract of land south of the Quapaw Tribe and north of the Ottawa Tribe. The original reservation goes from the Missouri border straight west to the Neosho (or Grand) River, encompassing a large part of the city of Miami before following the river north to the Kansas border. As with all other tribes and their collective holdings in the Indian or Oklahoma Territories, the Peoria reservation was allotted to tribal members in 1893. After falling victim to the federal government's tribal termination policies, the Peoria re-achieved federal recognition in 1978. The current Peoria headquarters is located just east of Miami near the intersection of Oklahoma Highway 10 and Interstate 44.

Tribal Music Traditions

While some tribal members participate in the Native American Church, and others attend Christian churches, the

Peoria people have embraced the stomp dance traditions of other area tribes, such as the Shawnee and Cherokee, as well as the intertribal powwow traditions that are so prominent in Oklahoma.

Live Music Venues

Ottawa-Peoria Cultural Center, 114 South Eight Tribes Trail, east of Miami at the intersection of Oklahoma Highway 10 and Interstate 44.

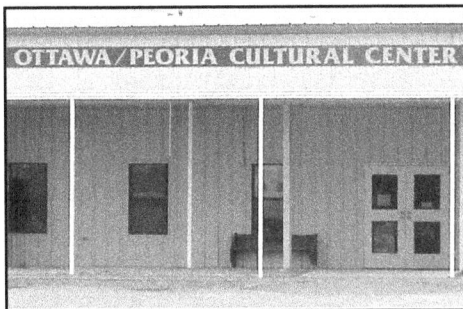

Peoria Powwow Grounds – 60610 E. 90 Road, Miami, OK, located three miles east of Miami, Oklahoma, and four miles south of Quapaw, Oklahoma, at County Road 137 and College Farm Road (E-90 Road). In case of rain, activities move to the Ottawa Peoria Cultural Center.

Peoria Casino and Event Center – Planned for a Labor Day, 2004, opening near the tribal complex east of Miami, the casino is to feature a 1,800-seat event center for concerts and other activities.

Annual Music Events

Annual Stomp Dance and Dinner – March, Cultural Center.
Annual Peoria Powwow – 4th weekend of June at the Peoria Powwow Grounds: gourd, stomp, and war dancing.

For More Information

Peoria Tribe of Indians of Oklahoma, 118 S. Eight Tribes Trail, P.O. Box, 1527, Miami, OK, 74355, www.peoriatribe.com (918) 540-2535

Ottawa Tribe of Oklahoma

Brief Tribal History

With its name deriving from the Algonquin word "adawe" (pronounced "uh-dah-way), meaning "to trade," or "to buy and sell," as the Ottawa were prominent trading

partners with the Chippewa, Potawatomi, and other Great Lakes tribes, the early historical record for the Ottawa places them at the mouth of the French River in what is now southern Michigan. In 1763 near present-day Detroit, the famous Ottawa chief, Pontiac, went to war against the British to keep them out of his section of Indian Country. By 1765, however, he made a peace treaty with the British, and bands of the tribe began moving south. In 1831, three groups of Ottawa people in Ohio ceded their lands to the United States for a reservation in Franklin County, Kansas, but the conditions were not favorable to the people and nearly half the tribe died within a few, short years.

As with the Peoria, Potawatomi, Iowa, and other current Oklahoma tribes removed to Kansas in the nineteenth century, the Ottawa were pressured to sell their lands and move to Indian Territory. In 1867, the Ottawa did just that and moved to a reservation in northeastern Oklahoma, the center of which is tiny Ottawa, Oklahoma, where the tribal headquarters is located. However, the center part of the city of Miami, on through to the Neosho (or Grand) River is in historic Ottawa Territory.

Tribal Music Traditions

Much like the Quapaw and Peoria, some Ottawa tribal members are participants in the Native American Church; however, most Ottawa people have embraced the intertribal powwow tradition.

Notable Musicians

Dr. Kevin Dawes, son of long-time Ottawa chief Charles Dawes, is well-known throughout Indian Country as a head singer at intertribal powwows.

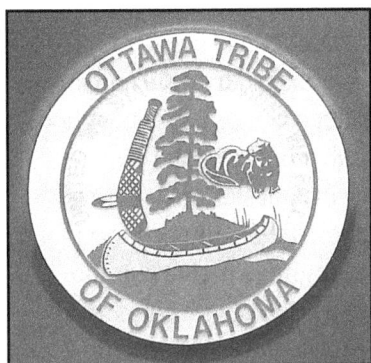

Annual Music Events

Since 1963, the Annual Ottawa Powwow has been held over Labor Day Weekend. Adair Park east of Miami, OK. Free and open to the public. Intertribal dancing.

For More Information

Ottawa Tribe of Oklahoma, P.O. Box 110, Miami, OK, 74355 (918) 540-1536

Miami

Established: 1891   **2000 Population:** 13,705

Brief History

Pronounced by locals "My-am-uh," the first chartered Indian Territory town began its modern history March 2, 1891, when Wayland C. Lykins, son of a missionary to the Peoria Indians, envisioned a community centered in the midst of vast grazing lands in the area. With ten American Indian tribes in the immediate area, Lykins benefited from the Federal Government's allotment program, which opened up "excess" tribal lands to settlers after each tribal member had been assigned their acreage of between 40 and 160 acres. The entrepreneur Lykins traveled to Washington, D.C. for the townsite's approval, and named it after the local Miami Tribe, now the Miami Tribe of Oklahoma.

Other tribes in the northeastern Oklahoma area around Miami include the Modoc, Ottawa, Peoria, Seneca-Cayuga, Wyandotte (often called Hurons in the history books), Quapaw, Eastern Shawnee, Shawnee Tribe of Oklahoma, and the Cherokee Nation of Oklahoma. Miami is also home to Northeastern Oklahoma A&M, established in 1919 and now the largest residential two-year college in the state. The school's football team produces a large number of Division I players who graduate "NEO" and become instant starters wherever they wind up. Of course, football being the popular sport that it is in Oklahoma, the town readily recognizes native son and 1969 Heisman Trophy winner Steve Owens with signs and street names, and Miami is also home to the astoundingly designed and historic Coleman Theatre Beautiful, which celebrated 75 years of continuous entertainment in April, 2004. What is not so publicly acknowledged is Miami being the birthplace of two musicians who rose to prominence in the 1970s as members of the Southern rock group Lynyrd Skynyrd: guitarist Steve Gaines and vocalist Cassie Gaines.

Notable Music History

Aside from the previously mentioned tribal music traditions covered elsewhere in the guide under those individual tribes, the most significant musicians to emerge from Miami include the Gaines siblings and blues guitarist Ace Moreland.

As members of southern rock group Lynyrd Skynyrd, guitarist Steve Earl Gaines (b. September 14, 1949 – d. October 20, 1977) and vocalist Cassie LaRue Gaines (b. January 9, 1948 – d. October 20, 1977) contributed significantly to the group's live concerts and recordings from 1976 to their tragic demise in 1977 when the band's plane crashed outside Gillsburg, Mississippi, on the way to a concert in Baton Rouge, Louisiana. Both Cassie and Steve were born in the northeastern corner of Oklahoma, in Miami, to Bud and LaRue Gaines. Even though she attended NEO A & M in Miami for two years, Cassie did not start singing professionally until she went to Memphis State University, where she graduated with a degree in physical education in 1975. Steve began playing guitar at fifteen, inspired after his father took him to see a 1965 performance by the Beatles in Kansas City. Upon returning to Miami, Steve's father bought him a guitar and Steve started his first group, the Ravens, in 1966, while still in high school. That group consisted of Steve on guitar and vocals, Archie Osborn (bass and vocals), Jerry Sanders (drums and vocals), and Johnny Burrows (guitar and vocals). After high school, Steve majored in art, first at Northeastern Oklahoma A & M, and then at Pittsburgh State College in Kansas.

In early 1972, Steve joined Detroit, essentially the Detroit Wheels without Mitch Ryder, which followed in the same blues rock mold popular among groups of the period, i.e., the Allman Brothers, the Marshall Tucker Band, and Skynyrd. After leaving the band Detroit, Steve and his wife, Teresa, moved to a farm in Seneca, Missouri, just across the Oklahoma border and not far from their home base of Miami, where they had their only child Corrina, named after a Taj Majal version of the song on which Oklahoma native Jesse Ed Davis played guitar.

In 1973 Steve formed Crawdad with John Seaburg (bass guitar and vocals), John Moss (guitar and vocals), Terry Emery (keyboards), and Ron Brooks (drums), performing everywhere from high school dances to the clubs and honky tonks in Oklahoma, Kansas, Arkansas, and Missouri. Steve's widow, now Teresa Gaines Rapp, has released two very insightful posthumous recordings from this period, *Okie Special* and *I Know A Little – Live*, both available though the Steve Gaines's website. *Okie Special* demonstrates Steve's varied influences, from Motown (Jr. Walker's "Road Runner") and funky fusion (Billy Cobham's "Crosswinds") to grooving blues (Chuck

Willis's "Snatch it Back and Hold It") and classic rock and roll (Chuck Berry's "No Money Down"). Two songs are also included on *Okie Special* from the Detroit group. Gaines's original composition, "Ain't No Good Life," later found on Skynyrd's *Street Survivors*, is also on *Okie Special*.

Another family-released disc indicating Steve Gaines's ultimate impact on Lynyrd Skynyrd can be found on *I Know a Little-Live*, recordings made by Gaines's groups Crawdad and Manalive in the early-to-mid-1970s. No dates are included on the compact disc, so determining their place in Gaines's development is difficult. However, the group's sound is so rooted in the popular southern rock of the time that Gaines's composition "I Know a Little" appears to have been written for Lynyrd Skynyrd even before they knew who Steve was. Again, Gaines's influences are prominent on the disc, with cover versions of songs by Freddie King, Big Joe Turner, Curtis Mayfield, and Bob Dylan. Cassie also makes a vocal appearance on one of Steve's songs, "People Comin' At Me."

In 1975 one of Cassie's friends from Memphis State, Jo Jo Billingsley, was a backup singer for Skynyrd. When the group told Billingsley they were looking for another singer, she asked Cassie to audition for the gig and she got it. Once on the job, Cassie found out Skynyrd also wanted to hire another guitarist to fatten up their sound after the relatively disappointing sales of their 1976 album *Gimme Back My Bullets* (MCA). She suggested her younger brother; and, when the group was playing in Kansas City, Cassie convinced them to let Steve sit in for one song. Singer Ronnie Van Zant agreed and instructed the soundman to cut Steve out of the mix if he could not keep up well enough. Gaines played slide on Jimmie Rodgers "T for Texas," impressed the whole band, and was invited to join the group.

The first Skynyrd recording to feature both Steve and Cassie Gaines is the Top 10 live album *One More for the Road* (MCA, 1976), which includes the famous fourteen-minute jamathon version of "Free Bird." Back in the studio with a renewed sense of purpose and a fresh injection from Steve Gaines's guitar work and compositions, Skynyrd recorded *Street Survivors* (MCA, 1977). Two of Steve's songs he had been playing for years with his other groups, "Ain't No Good Life" and "I Know a Little," appear on the album, and he co-wrote two new songs with vocalist Van Zant, "You Got That Right" and "I Never Dreamed." Steve's trademark "popping Stratocaster" style can be heard on the band's cover of Merle Haggard's "Honky Tonk Night Time Man," and Cassie's backup vocals are also prominent on the best-selling Lynyrd Skynyrd album. While *Street Survivors* returned the group to the international stardom, three days after the album's release the band's plane crashed due to a seemingly negligent decision by the pilot about having enough fuel in the aircraft, killing Cassie, Steve, Ronnie Van Zant, and the band's manager, Dean Kilpatrick. Ironically, the album cover for *Street Survivors* included a picture of the group engulfed in flames, and the record was taken off the market in the U.S. to have the cover photo replaced. European releases maintained the original cover.

Periodically, more material from Gaines's career has been made available. In 1988, MCA Records released a Steve Gaines solo album, *One in the Sun*, culled from tapes he had recorded with producer John Ryan at the Capricorn Studio in Macon, Georgia, and Leon Russell's Church Studio in Tulsa. Enlisting his old band mates from Crawdad to back him up, the out-of-print album is clearly a work in progress, with the Capricorn tracks recorded "live" and the Church tracks pieced together track-by-track. Steve's promise as a guitarist and vocalist in the southern rock boogie blues genre is obvious on the album's lead-off track "Give It to Get It," a song later covered by Cherokee guitarist Ace Moreland (also from Miami). Released in 2003, the Manalive recordings made at the Sun Studios in Memphis are available only through the Steve Gaines website. Also in 2003, the Rock and Roll Hall of Fame in Cleveland, Ohio exhibited Steve's Fender Stratocaster guitar as part of the Lynyrd Skynyrd exhibit.

With Steve Gaines as an inspiration in his hometown, Cherokee blues guitarist James "Ace" Moreland (b. Miami, OK, d. Feb. 8, 2003) recorded four searing albums of blues in for Ichiban, Wild Dog, and King Snake Records, and worked as a sideman for notable blues artists such as Sonny Rhodes.

Included in Moreland's catalogue is the Cherokee history based song "Indian Giver" on the CD *Give It To Get It* (King Snake, 2000), an album title taken from the previously mentioned Steve Gaines song.

Historic Music Sites

The Coleman Theatre Beautiful has been providing Miami-area residents with entertainment since April 18, 1929, when 1,600 patrons paid $1.00 each to see a vaudeville show and a "talkie" movie titled *The Dummy*. With its stained glass panels, carved mahogany staircase, and 1,000-pound chandelier, the Coleman Theatre was placed on the National Register of Historic Places in 1983. Also, in 1996 the theater's original pipe organ, the "Mighty Wurlitzer," returned to the Coleman restored, refurbished, and enhanced. Miami citizens donated all of the $85,000 used to repurchase and repair the organ, thus re-creating the only theatre in Oklahoma (and one of the few in the United States) with its original pipe organ in its original setting.

Currently, the Community Concerts organization and Miami Little Theatre group use the auditorium, as do local churches and public schools for their plays, pageants, and concerts. Tours of this grand old show business palace are free and conducted Tuesday through Friday from 10 a.m. to 4 p.m., or call (918) 540-2425, extension 454, for an appointment.

Music Stores

Miami Music
  122 N. Main
  (918) 542-2280

Outback Music
  309 N. Main
  (918) 542-4720

Annie P. Annie (far right) and her band rock the Blue Door
Lounge, 900 E. Steve Owens Boulevard in Miami, 2004.

Tulsa's Stonehorse performing in 2004 at R & B Country
in Miami on 111 S. Treaty Road .

Annual Musical Events

Designs of Autumn Arts and Music Festival, third weekend in
September, Main Street, (918) 542-9803.

Of Additional Interest

Dobson Museum, 110 "A" Street SW, Open Sunday,
  Wednesday, Friday, 1 p.m. to 4 p.m. Free, (918) 542-5388
Eight Tribes Gift Shop, 21 N. Eight Tribes Trail,
  (918) 542-5388

For More Information about Miami

Miami Area Convention and Visitors Bureau, 111 N. Main,
  Box 760, 74355, (918) 542-1590, www.visitmiamiok.com

Miami Tribe of Oklahoma

Brief Tribal History

Tracing their modern origins to the current area of Green Bay,
Wisconsin, the Miami tribe migrated into the Ohio Valley where
they made homes in parts of Illinois, Indiana, and Ohio. The
Miami tribe fought
throughout the Great
Lakes region between
the 1650s and the
1840s. In 1840, the
Miami agreed to cede
their lands for a
reservation in the
West, which is
manifested today in
Miami County,
Kansas. After about twenty years on the reservation, the
Kansas Territory government deemed the Miami lands too rich
for the tribe to occupy solely. Subsequently, in 1867, tribal
members could take an allotment and become a citizen of
Kansas, or move to Indian Territory where they were to be
incorporated with the Peoria and affiliated tribes. While some
Miami did become affiliated with the Peoria, the majority
declined and formed the Miami Tribe of Oklahoma.

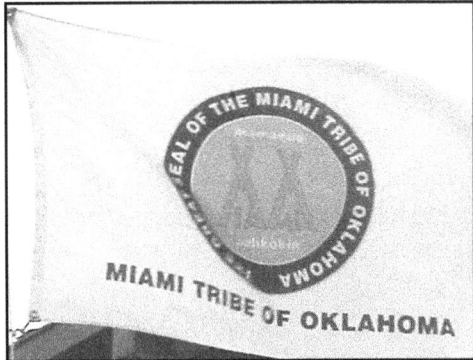

Tribal Music Traditions

With a current enrollment of a little over 2,000 members, the Miami Tribe sponsors an annual stomp dance in conjunction with an art market in the winter months, and also have hosted an annual powwow since 1999 at the Miami Fair Grounds in Miami. Held the first weekend of June, the powwow features gourd dancing, intertribal dancing, and a stomp dance on both Friday and Saturday night. Contact: Walesah (918) 542-1445

For More Information about the Miami Tribe

www.miamination.com

Modoc Tribe

Brief Tribal History

The modern history of the Modoc Tribe begins with them separating from their Klamath kin in northern California and southern Oregon. The word "modoc"

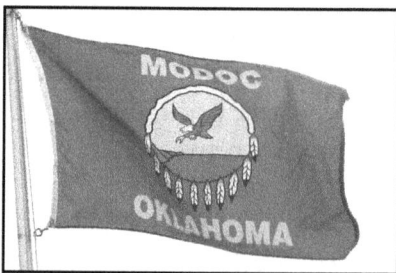

in the Klamath language means "southern ones." After separating, the tribe ultimately clashed with the logging and mining culture of the Americans who came West in pursuit of "golden" opportunities. The end result led to the Modoc Wars, which in turn sent those who were not executed by the U.S. Government to Indian Territory. Currently, the smallest tribe among those in Oklahoma at a little more than 200 members, the Modoc make their presence felt in Miami with a gaming facility, The Stables.

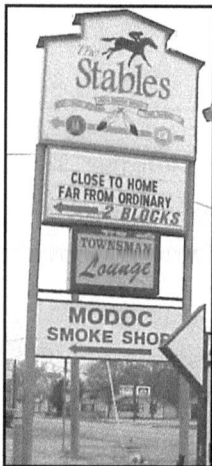

For More Info call (918) 542-1190.

Cherokee Nation of Oklahoma

Driving south out of Miami, travelers cross into the Cherokee Nation of Oklahoma, a tribal jourisdiction of 6,964 square miles in which more than 460,000 people live. No attempt will be made to summarize Cherokee history beyond their modern origins in the area of western North Carolina, throughout modern-day Kentucky, and Tennessee, and in parts of Alabama, Georgia, South Carolina, and the Virginias. Even people with the most casual knowledge of American history, know about the forced removal of the Cherokee and other Southeastern tribes to Indian Territory over what is known as the "trail where they cried," or the "long walk," in the 1830s.

Traveling through Oklahoma, many opportunities exist to learn about the Cherokees, and a stop at the Will Rogers Memorial in Claremore is a standard stop on the Route, but one must deviate from Oklahoma Route 66 to reach Tahlequah, the capitol of the Cherokee Nation, which takes about an hour. The trip can be quite educational, with a visit to the Cherokee Heritage Center in Tahlequah, or the capitol complex that features a gift shop with Cherokee arts, crafts, and music. When travelers reach Catoosa, where Route 66 and Interstate 44 merge, they will see the Cherokee Nation Casino and Resort (picture at right) scheduled for completion in

September, 2004. For more information on Cherokee music, see the *Oklahoma Music Guide* or www.cherokee.org.

Tribal Music Traditions

The active Cherokee musical traditions include the cermonial and social songs and dances known in English as "stomp dances" (pictured at right). The hymns resulting from two centuries of interaction with Christianity are most popularly manifested in award-winning recordings by the Cherokee National Youth Choir. The revitilization of the river cane flute, originally used for courting purposes, now also enjoys wide attention in the new age music realm and, in contemporary American Indian music, with the flute accented by reverb, echo, and/or other instruments. Also, the Cherokee fiddle style is unique with its own tunings and interpretations of traditional Anglo "mountain music" fiddle. Cherokee fiddler Sam O'Fields (pictured at right) was still active in 2004.

In popular music, pioneering electric guitarist, Nokie Edwards of The Ventures, is of Cherokee descent, and Leo Feathers, born in Stilwell, played guitar for Leon Russell, Willie Nelson, and Bonnie Raitt. According to Elvis Presley's website, his maternal great-great-grandmother Morning Dove White (b.1800-d.1835) was a full-blooded Cherokee. Tulsa Sound alum Jack Dunham is enrolled Cherokee, as was Miami-born blues guitarist Ace Moreland. Other pop musicians who have been allied with Cherokee descendancy include Jimi Hendrix, Hank Williams, Willie Nelson, Loretta Lynn, and Rita Coolidge.

Annual Music Events

Many events are held throughout the year in Tahlequah, and in other places around the Cherokee Nation. The best time to catch everything going on at once is during the Labor Day Holiday celebration at which time one can hear hymns, the fiddle, stomp dances (no cameras allowed), and attend a powwow at the Cherokee Nation Powwow Grounds.

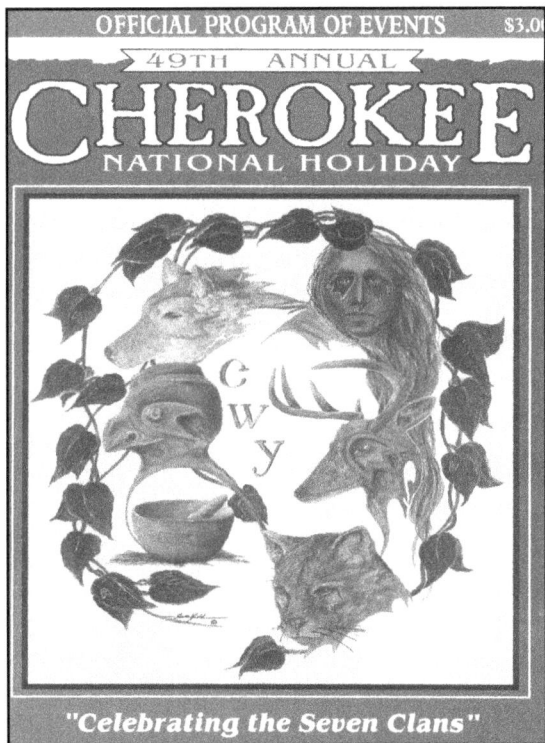

"Celebrating the Seven Clans"

The Cherokee Trail of Tears Drama focuses on the joys and sorrows of a single Cherokee family and their children for the past 150 years -- from the Trail of Tears to the present day. Opens in June and runs through Labor Day Weekend. Contact the Cherokee Heritage Center at 918-456-6007.

For More Information on the Cherokee Nation

www.cherokee.org

Narcissa

Established: 1902

2000 Population: 100

The best opportunity for live music in this rural community is at the local First Baptist Church of Narcissa (pictured at right). Incidentally, about 10 miles west of Narcissa is the community of Bluejacket, notable as the hometown of Fern Holland, the attorney and women's rights activist who lost her life in Iraq in early 2004 while working with Iraqi women to improve their status there.

Afton

Established: 1886

2000 Population: 1,118

Live Music Venue:

Afton's proximity to Grand Lake of the Cherokees provides ample traffic to support a small tavern, the Kountry Kitchen Bar and Grill, that features live music on most weekends.

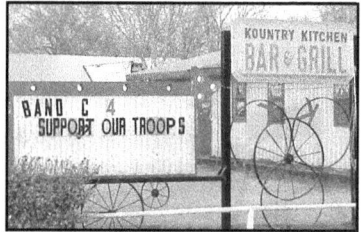

Notable Music Figure: Monica Taylor of the country folk duo, the Farm Couple, lives near Afton.

Museum with a Route 66 Focus:

Afton Station, 12 SE 1st St., 918-382-9465

For More Information about Afton:

Afton Chamber of Commerce, (918) 786-2289

Afton City Hall, (918) 257-4304

Vinita

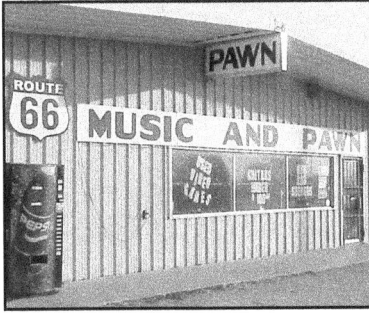

Established: 1871

2000 Population: 6,472

Local History Source
Eastern Trails Museum, 215 W. Illinois, Nice collection relating to Vinita's early days. (918) 256-2115

Notable Music Figures

Vinita is home to local country music singer, songwriter, and guitarist Clint Walker, born March 14th, 1975. Clint has opened for David Frizell, Hank Thompson, and Jerry Reed, as well as performing at the Grove Opry as a headliner. Another Vinita group is the Southern rock-leaning band, Fully Loaded.

For Vinyl Collectors

Vinita has several antique and collectible stores that occasionally have vinyl. For starters, try the Vinita Antique Mall for starters at 127 S. Wilson, Maxine's Collectors Palace at 113 E. Canadian, or Gene's Collectibles at 223 S. Wilson.

Annual Musical Events

The World's Largest Calf Fry Festival and Cook Off, held the second Friday and Saturday of each September, includes country music concert and nightly dances.
Summer Fest - first weekend of August - features live music.

For More Information about Vinita

Chamber of Commerce, www.vinita.com, or (918) 256-7133.

White Oak

Established: 1898 as a Frisco Railroad community
Population: No census figures exist.

Notable Music History

The most significant music in the White Oak area is the ceremonial music of the Shawnee Tribe of Oklahoma, formerly known as the Loyal Shawnee, whose ceremonial grounds is not far from the unincorporated community of White Oak.

Victoria Dougherty, born in the White Oak community in 1918, and a member of the Loyal Shawnee Tribe, is featured in State Arts Council of Oklahoma publication, *Remaining Ourselves: Music and Tribal Memory* (1995), a book about some of the surviving tradtional music in contemporary tribal communities. In the feature on her, Dougherty describes the sacred use of tobacco and sings a "Tobacco Lullaby," a song her mother sang while warming "medicine" milk for a colicky baby, and similtaneously blowing tobocco smoke into the milk while stirring it.

For Vinyl Collectors

Along with a dizzying display of hand made, wrought iron ornaments and statues,The Little Tin Barn Flea Market, right on Route 66 in White Oak, also has a rotating collection of vinyl, both 78s and 33s, some of which may be hard to get to, so slow down and ask to see them. Call (918) 256-5415 for more information from owner Bertha Miller.

Shawnee Tribe of Oklahoma

Brief Tribal History

The Shawnee people are
historically linked to the Ohio
Valley until the point of their
contact, and ultimately, their
military engagements with the
British, French, and
Americans. Subsequently, the
tribe endured similar hardships
to other area tribes who either migrated out of necessity, or
were removed to Indian Territory, first in Kansas, and then in
present-day Oklahoma. Three bands of Shawnee currently call
Oklahoma home: the Eastern Shawnee located in eastern
Ottawa County just shy of the Oklahoma border near Seneca,
Missouri; the Absentee Shawnee, also known as Tecumseh's
band, located near Shawnee, Oklahoma; and, the Shawnee
Tribe of Oklahoma, formerly known as the Loyal Shawnee
because of their service to the Union Army, and who received
their individual federal recognition as a tribe in 2002.

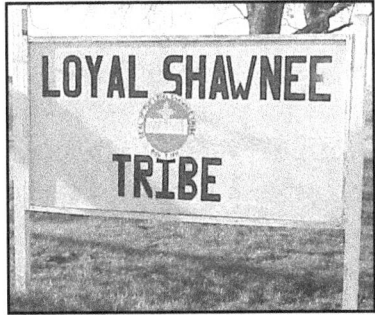

Tribal Music Traditions

The Shawnee Tribe of Oklahoma maintains their ceremonial
traditions at a rural ceremonial grounds. These traditions are
discussed extensively in James Howard's book, *Shawnee!: The
Ceremonialism of a Native American Tribe and Its Cultual
Background.* In 2000, the tribe began hosting an annual
powwow at the Peoria Powwow grounds, 60610 East 90 Rd.,
three miles east of Miami, Oklahoma, near the intersection with
County Road 137. Held the third weekend of each September,
on Friday and Saturday, the powwow features gourd dancing,
contest powwow dancing, stomp dance contests, and the
Shawnee-unique Potato Dance on Saturday night.

Notable Musicians

Aside from George Valliere, Jr., mentioned in the Quapaw entry, and Victoria Dougherty, mentioned in the White Oak entry, James Squirrel is one of the most visible, enrolled Shawnee singers of both powwow songs and stomp dances. In addition to his traditional singing at the White Oak Ceremonial Grounds, Squirrel can be heard regularly at powwows and social stomp dances throughout Oklahoma, as can Absentee Shawnee Troy Littleaxe, Senior, both of whom have recorded for Indian House Records on *Stomp Dance Blues with English Lyrics: A Tribute to Johnna* (IH 3101).

James Squirrel (first from left), and Troy Littleaxe, Sr. (second from left) are well-known singers at both powwows and stomp dances throughout Oklahoma.

For More Information about the Shawnee Tribe of Oklahoma

Shawnee Tribal Office: (918) 542-2441.

Chelsea

Established: 1870

2000 Population: 2,136

Notable Music History

Popular legend often recounts that, sometime in 1928, the famous Oklahoma humorist Will Rogers, heard Gene Autry singing in the Chelsea railroad depot and suggested the 21-year-old singing telegraph operator head to New York and try to make it there on radio. Gene thought about it while continuing to play locally for about a year, and then took advantage of a free Frisco railway pass to New York City that put him on his way to being one of the great popular culture icons of 20th century U.S. entertainment.

For Vinyl Collectors

The Little Tin Barn 2 (pictured at right) on Route 66 east of downtown at 422 Walnut, features a rotating collection of used 33 and 78 rpm vinyl. Call (918) 244-0461 for information.

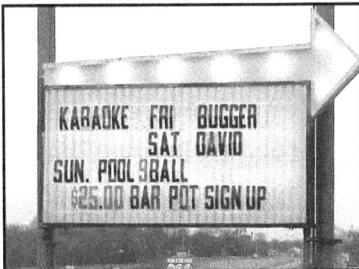

Live Music Venues

The Longhorn Tavern, west of Chelsea, features karaoke singing on Friday and Saturday nights.

For More Information

Chelsea Area Chamber of Commerce: 618 Pine, (918) 789-2220

Bushyhead

Established: 1898, named for Dennis W. Bushyhead, Chief of the Cherokee Nation from 1879-1887.

2000 Population: 1,203

Live Music Venues

Like many small communities, the local church is the best place to hear live music each week, usually on Sunday mornings, Sunday nights, and Wednesday evenings.

Foyil

Established: 1890

2000 Population: 234

Tourist Notes:

Foyil is known primarily for being the home of Andy Payne, the winner of the 84-day, 2400-mile International Continental Footrace in 1928. A long time Route 66 icon, Totem Pole Park is 4 miles east of Foyil on State Highway 28A.

FRIENDLY FOYIL BAPTIST Church

THE SPEED YOU ARE GOING IS NOT AS IMPORTANT AS THE DIRECTION HEADED

Live Music Venues

Same as Bushyead and Narcissa, Foyil's most active music scene is in its churches.

For More Information

Foyil City Hall, (918) 342-9525

Sequoyah

Established: 1871

2000 Population: 671

Local Music

Aside from the area's churches, adventurous travelers of the appropriate age can enjoy a cold beverage, and some local flavor at Jack's Place on Route 66.

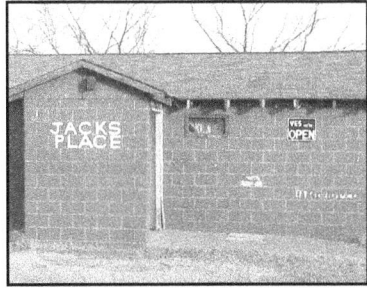

Claremore

Established: In the early 1800s, named for Osage Chief Clermont.

2000 Population: 15, 873

Notable Music History

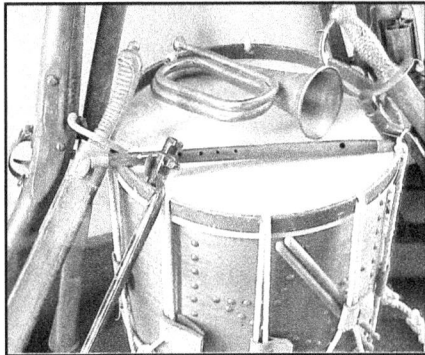

While Claremore is regularly recognized as a necessary Route 66 stop because of the Will Rogers Memorial and Museum, as well as the J.M. Davis Arms and Historical Museum which houses several antique instruments and music boxes (pictured above), musically inclined travelers will be interested in additional music history sites, as well as the musicians who have come from Claremore to enjoy great success such as Patti Page and Jim Keltner, Jack Anquoe, Jr., Mark McClurg, and, more recently, Nokose Foley.

Notable Music Figures

Patti Page   Popular Singer

Born: November 8, 1927, in Claremore

Notability: One of the pure superstar voices of 20th century popular music, Patti Page (right) has sold more than 100 million records. With fifteen certified gold records, Page will always be remembered for her mega-crossover hit of 1950, "Tennessee Waltz," the most successful single in country music history with ten million sold, and to a lesser extent for her novelty song recorded for a children's album, "The Doggie in the Window." Page has charted 111 songs on the pop, country, and R & B charts, and her hit "Confess" is the first song in music history to feature a vocalist performing both lead and backup vocals via overdubbing in the studio. Patti Page has won a Grammy Award and was inducted into the Oklahoma Music Hall of Fame's inaugural class of 1997.

Jim Keltner   All-World Drummer

Born: Claremore

Notability: Known as one of the world's best drummers, Jim Keltner's span of session work spans from 1969 to the present day. A partial, short list of his staggering credits include recordings with John Lennon, George Harrison, Leon Russell, Barbara Streisand, Steve Miller, Arlo Guthrie, the Bee Gees, Bob Dylan, James Taylor, Dolly Parton, Leonard Cohen, Steely Dan, J.J. Cale, Charlie Watts, Neil Diamond, Earl Scruggs, and Roy Orbison.

Jack "Jackie" Anquoe, Jr.   (Kiowa/Cherokee)
Intertribal Powwow Singer
Born: Claremore Indian Hospital
Notability: An intertribal powwow singer since the 1970s with
the Redland Singers, led by Tony Arkeketa, and the Grayhorse
Singers, which is led by his Anquoe's father, Jack Anquoe Sr.,
several recordings featuring "Jackie" exist, as well as others
released by the Anquoe family of singers. CDs and tapes of the
Grayhorse Singers can be found most readily at Lyon's Indian
Store on Route 66 in Tulsa.

Mark McClurg   Country Fiddler
Born: Claremore
Notability: A twelve-year veteran of Alan Jackson's band, the
Strayhorns, as well a long-time member of the Claremore-based
country group, Stonehorse, McClurg teamed up with another
Oklahoman, Wade Hayes, to form the popular country group
McHayes in 2003.

Nokose Foley Muscogee (Creek)   Drummer
Born: November 30, 1994, at the Claremore Indian Hospital
Notability: With his recording of an intertribal powwow song,
"Grand Entry," for the Delicious Militia's 1998 country-rock
album, *Whatever Happened to the Banjo Girl?,* Nokose's

track appeared on Radio Shanghai's Top
Ten in 1999, one place above Atari
Teenage Riot on the March playlist of
that year. A fancy dancer who has been
singing powwow music since he was 2,
Nokose began studying the trap set
formally in 2003. Additionally, his work
as a Route 66 detective and enthusiast
inspired this book immeasurably.

Historic Sites with a Musical Focus

The Lynn Riggs Memorial Museum chronicles the life of playwright Lynn Riggs, author of *Green Grow the Lilacs*, the play that forms the basis for Rodgers and Hammerstein's famous musical *Oklahoma!*, the first major musical to have a plot line threading through the musical numbers. Open Monday through Friday, 9am to 4pm, Sunday 1pm to 5pm, June to August; group tours by appointment at (918) 627-2716.

Music Store
Claremore Music on Rt. 66
(918) 342-4044

For Vinyl Collectors
Claremore has several antique stores along Will Rogers Blvd. that feature a rotating selection of vinyl 78s and 33s.

Contemporary music fans will find The Beat Goes On, in the Ne-Mar Center just a block north of Route 66 on Hwy 20, a good place to stock up on current compact discs and tapes, as well as browse the used vinyl bin.

Live Music Venues

Along with the campus of Rogers State University where occasional concerts take place in the campus auditorium, the Mustard Tree (right) on old Route 66 was one of the area's most popular Christian Rock performance spaces until relocating to Tulsa in late summer 2004.

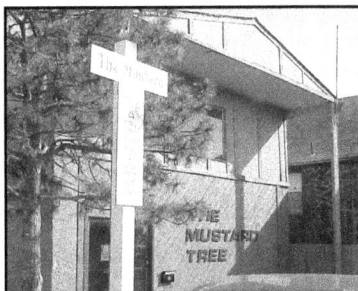

Annual Musical Events

Annual Bluegrass and Chili Festival, 2nd weekend of September, featuring free bluegrass, country, and Christian music concerts by national and regional performers. (918) 341-2818

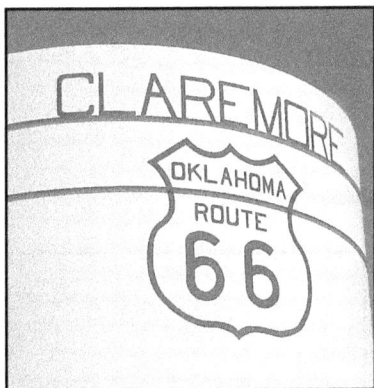

June's Country Fever in Pryor is Oklahoma's Largest Outdoor Country Music Festival. (888) 597-7827, www.countryfeverfest.com

For More Information

Claremore Convention and Visitors Bureau
419 W. Will Rogers Blvd., Claremore, 74017
(918) 341-8688 or
www.claremore.org

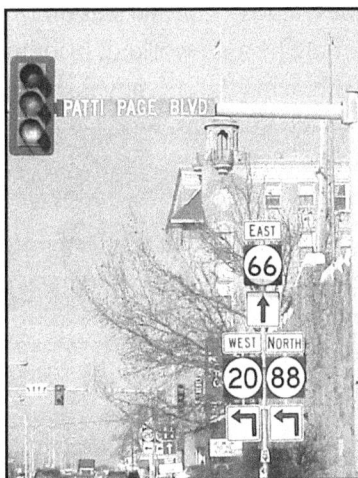

Verdigris

Established: 1880   *2000 Population:* 22,077

Annual Musical Events Annual Bluegrass Jam,
   1st weekend of June, Verdigris Elementary School
   Verdigris Jazz Festival, September

For More Information

Verdigris Chamber of Commerce (918) 341-4253 or
www.verdigrisok.org

Catoosa

Established: 1882

2000 Population: 5,449

Historic Sites with a Musical Focus

   The Catoosa Historical
Museum features many items
related to the town's past, but
also includes an interesting Gene
Autry exhibit that displays a rare
photo of Autry performing at
the Catoosa railroad station,
where he also worked, prior to
embracing the cowboy fashion
that he would eventually
make so famous that a
person couldn't be
considered a country
singer if not wearing a
cowboy hat. Located
at 207 N. Cherokee,
the museum is open
Tuesday and Friday
from 10am to 3pm.

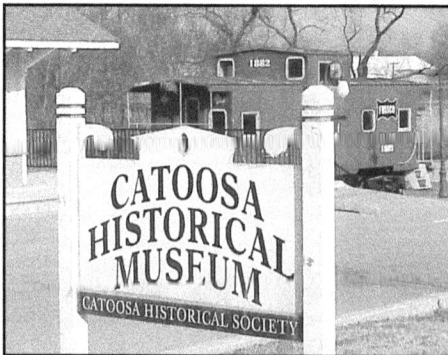

Live Music Venue

For live country music on the weekends, visit Redneck Kountry, just across I-44 from the Cherokee Nation Casino on Route 66.

For More Information

Catoosa Chamber of Commerce, 750 S. Cherokee #M, 74015 , (918) 266-6042

Muscogee (Creek) Nation

Brief History

With one traditional story explaining their origins in the West when the earth's mouth opened during an earthquake, and a subsequent journey toward the sunrise where they eventually created the highly evolved and structured mound building culture of the Southeastern United States, the tribe now known as the Muscogee (Creek) Nation, with its contemporary headquarters in Okmulgee and total territory comprising more than 4,700 square miles, began arriving in Indian Territory in 1828 after leaving their pre-historic homelands of Alabama, Georgia, Florida, and South Carolina as a result of the United States government's removal policy of the early 19th century. Once travelers leave Catoosa on Route 66/I-44 and begin heading into Tulsa, they enter the modern Muscogee (Creek) Nation.

Tribal Music Traditions

With several active ceremonial grounds where traditional Muscogee music is very much alive, a deep Christian hymn singing tradition that is more than two hundred years old, and several contemporary musicians who have made significant contributions to the popular music and intertribal

powwow music worlds, the Muscogee (Creek) Nation is a musically rich and diverse tribe whose contributions to world music illustrate both the preservation of ancient songs under oppressive circumstances, and more modern music that has evolved due to cross-cultural contact between Muscogee people and Americans of African and European descent.

Of particular interest to contemporary students, fans, and scholars of American music, Muscogee ceremonial music may have been heretofore overlooked as a possible contributor to the development of American jazz. Alert listeners to Muscogee ceremonial songs, often called "stomp dances" in English, will hear the women "shell shakers" keep a rhthym that is very much like the "swinging eights" of jazz. Given the historical interaction between the Muscogee and people of African descent, as manifested intensely in some Muscogee Christian hymns, one should not be surprised to imagine the possible connections between the two forms of music that both rose out of the American South. For excellent recordings of stomp dances, hear *Stomp Dance Songs of the Muscogee Nation* (IH3009)

Muscogee hymns are also very significant for Creek and Seminole people who sing them in mostly rural Baptist and Methodist churches dotted throughout the Creek Nation. The hymns extol the hope necessary to make it to the promised land, and serve the double purpose of also commemorating the removal of Muscogee people to Indian Territory.

While both Muscogee traditional and Christian musicians continue practicing their particular forms, other Muscogee people have moved into American popular music realms, as well as the intertribal powwow world, and have also made modern recordings of traditional instruments, such as the river cane flute.

Notable Musicians

Several Muscogee people have made contributions to American popular music. Jim Pepper (Muscogee/Kaw) successfully merged American Indian traditional music with jazz, most notably on his "Witchi Tai To," which hit both the Top 40 and jazz charts in 1969. Jesse Ed Davis (Kiowa/Comanche/Muscogee) was one of the most in-demand rock session guitarists of the 1970s, playing with the like of John Lennon, George Harrison, Eric Clapton, and many others. Joy Harjo (b. Tulsa, 1951) has also released two albums of music with her own spoken-word poetry, singing, and alto and soprano saxophone work. Muscogee rapper and musician Julian B. has recorded two albums of better than average rap, with lyrics that invoke the Muscogee language, and music that ranges between smooth R&B and outspoken, activist-oriented raps about American Indian history.

Muscogee musicians have also made notable contributions to contemporary music of the powwow arena. Since the early 1970s, three brothers, Wayne Coser (b. Okmulgee), George Coser, Jr. (b. Tulsa), and Pete G. Coser (b. Okmulgee, and pictured at right), have been members of the intertribal Redland Singers, a drum group noted for being the very first to bring the high-pitched style of northern singing to Oklahoma powwows.

Subsequently, Pete Coser's son, Pete "Petey" Robert George Coser, began singing with the Redland Singers as a youngster, and currently is a member of Thunderhorse, a northern-style group with two albums on the Arbor label, *Riding the Storm* (AR-113820) and *Native America* (AR-11592). In the southern singing style genre, G.C. Tsouhlarakis (Muscogee/Navajo) and Sam Cook (Muscogee/Pawnee) have recorded for Canyon Records with the Grammy-nominated drum group, Young Bird.

Another recent trend is the revitalization of the river cane flute for recording purposes in the genre of new age music, or contemporary American Indian music. The most recent success in this area is John "Yafke" Timothy, whose independent recording, *Inutska*, landed Timothy a national recording and distribution deal with Oyate Records. Timothy is the curator of the Ataloa Lodge Museum at Bacone College in Muskogee.

Historic Sites with a Musical Focus

Muscogee (Creek) Nation Council House
106 W. 6th Street, Okmulgee, 74447, (918) 756-2324

Annual Music Events

Given the extremely diverse history of music in the Muscogee (Creek) Nation and among its people, one can learn a lot in a short amount of time at the Annual Creek Nation Festival and Rodeo, held the third weekend of June each year on the tribal grounds, north of Okmulgee on U.S. Highway 75. Along with the rodeo and softball and track tournaments, the annual festival always features a gospel concert and exhibition stomp dance, but also includes American Indian popular and country music artists of national stature, as well as an intertribal powwow.

For More Information on the Muscogee Nation

www.muscogeenation-nsn.gov or (918) 756-8700

In the 1940s Tulsa was still in its massive oil refinery production phase. Route 66 crosses the Arkansas River (upper left).

Tulsa

Established: 1836
2000 Population: 393,049

Notable Music History

Tulsa's place in the American music landscape is giant. Practically no genre has been unplucked, unblown, unthumped, or unsung by musicians associated with Tulsa.

The first modern music of the area is that of the Osage, whose historic buffalo trails ranged near present day Tulsa. The Osage war dance ceremonies known as "In-Lon-Shka" fill the Osage country with traditional music each year summer. While some of north Tulsa is considered part of the Osage Reservation, the northeast section of Tulsa is in the Cherokee Nation, and the southern and southeastern part of Tulsa is in the Muscogee (Creek) Nation, so those music styles would also be considered part of Tulsa's overall musical palette, as is the

intertribal powwow world. Both the Tulsa Powwow, started in the 1940s, and the Intertribal Indian Club of Tulsa's Powwow of Champions (pictured above), have become two of the most prominent urban powwows in the United States.

After American Indian music, Tulsa's music history follows the course of American music as a whole in the 20th century, providing some extremely important contributions along the way. Covered extensively in the *Oklahoma Music Guide*, Tulsa's jazz history ranges from past greats such as saxophonist Earl Bostic (b. 1913), bassist Cecil McBee (b.1935), and the trumpeter who became an inspiration to Miles Davis, Howard McGhee (b. 1918), to contemporary jazz figures such as Wayman Tisdale, Grady Nichols, and Tommy Crook.

Of course, Tulsa would not be Tulsa if it weren't for the "House That Bob Built," also known as the Cain's Ballroom, located at 423 N. Main. That Bob would be Bob Wills, whose Texas Playboys merged country, pop, jazz, blues, and mariachi into Western swing, a dancehall music meant to help partyers forget about the depression, or celebrate

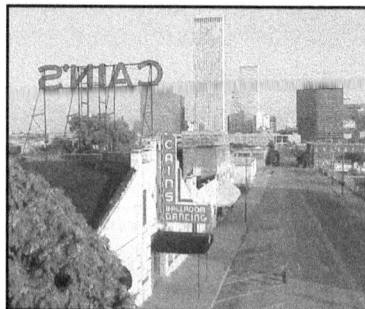

the end of World War II. Wills became famous via 50,000 watt KVOO, the "Voice of Oklahoma," heard throughout much of the midwest , southwest, and West.

If jazz was Tulsa's music in the 1920s, and Western swing owned the scene for the 1930s and through the 1940s, rock and roll raised its head in the 1950s. Tulsa's music scene of the Elvis-era jetted several players to national status, to include Flash Terry, Jack Dunham, Leon Russell, David Gates, Elvin Bishop, J.J. Cale, Junior Markham and Tommy Crook. Additional musicians such as drummers Jim Keltner and Chuck Blackwell, bassist Carl Radle, keyboardist Rocky Frisco, and guitarist Leo Feathers contributed to this environment that produced what has come to be known as the "Tulsa Sound." Many more musicians contributed to the city's music scene, and interested readers can consult the *Oklahoma Music Guide*, or the *Tulsa World*'s online archives for more details.

By all accounts, the Tulsa Sound is a musical stew of country, blues, rock, and occasionally jazz, that has its sources in the multi-faceted "Okie Jazz" of Bob Wills, the rich R&B history of Tulsa, and the teenage musicians of the 1950s who embraced the burgeoning rock and roll movement while infusing it with their own Tulsa twang and earthy blues. What later becomes known as the Tulsa Sound of the 1970s might best be described as 50s rockers slowing down, maturing, starting families and changing priorities, which is reflected in the more relaxed style of music manifested most directly by Leon Russell's easy-paced recordings of the early 1970s. Eric Clapton's 1974 tribute to Cale, *Slowhand* (MCA), with a rhythm section of Oklahomans Jamie Oldaker and Carl Radle, as well as Dire Straits *Sultans of Swing* (Sire, 1978), are both just mainstream popular music catching up to Tulsa's hip hybrid of blues, country, and rock. In the 1990s, Steve Ripley's Tractors mined the same vein for their multi-platinum success, and by 2004, periodic Tulsa Sound reunions, or independent appearances by those musicians drew appreciative audiences.

Leon Russell

On the strength of his massive popular success in the early 1970s, Leon Russell returned to Tulsa where he purchased the First Church of God at Third and Trenton. Russell converted the building into the now-famous Church Studio, currently owned and operated by Steve Ripley of the Tractors. The Church Studio provided a nexus through which some of rock's biggest performers channeled their recording sessions away from the microcopic pressures of New York or L.A. Bob Dylan and J.J. Cale recorded there in the early 1970s; native Tulsan Howard Twilley recorded his 1975 Top 20 hit, "I'm on Fire," in the building; and the GAP Band experienced some of their earlieest recordings in the Church Studio.

The GAP Band (Formed in 1967, Tulsa, OK)

Leaning on influences ranging from Parliament-Funkadelic and Sly and the Family Stone to Earth, Wind, and Fire, The GAP Band, comprised of multi-instrumentalist brothers Ronnie, Charlie, and Robert Wilson (all Tulsa natives), surfaced as one of the most popular R & B groups of the 1980s. With fifteen Top 10 R & B hits, the group has become a perennial favorite of sample-happy hip hop and R & B artists looking for a fat bass lines, smooth vocal hooks, and funky beats. The brothers grew up performing in their father's Pentecostal church in Tulsa

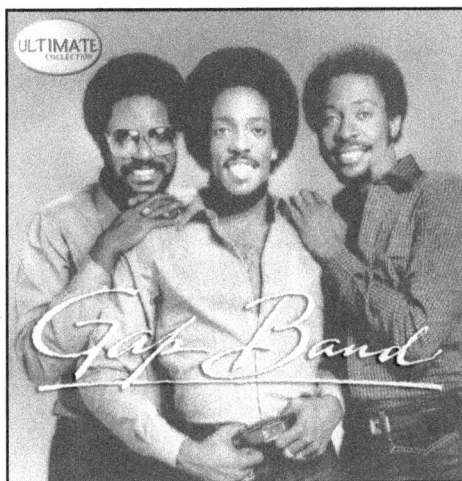

where their mother was a pianist, and where they sang every Sunday. All three brothers took piano lessons, and their parents demanded they practice at home. Ronnie, the oldest, started a group when he was fourteen and eventually recruited his younger brothers to play in the band they named after streets in the heart of Tulsa's historic African-American business district: Greenwood, Archer and Pine. After playing various clubs around Tulsa, they provided bass, horns, and vocals to Leon Russell's album *All That Jazz*. Subsequently, after Russell signed the band to record their first album for his Shelter label, *Magician's Holiday* (1974), they moved to Los Angeles where they began a successful career in R&B and pop music.

Numerous compilations document he GAP Band's career: *Gap Gold: The Best of the Gap Band* (Mercury, 1985); and a best-of collection via Mercury's *20th Century Masters Series*.

In 2001 Hip-O released *Ultimate Collection*, a thorough summary of the GAP Band's greatest hits with extensive liner notes, while Ark 21 released *Love at Your Fingertips*, featuring a few new tunes, live recordings, and several remixes of "You Dropped a Bomb on Me."

A continuation of Tulsa's music history in the 1970s includes power pop beacon Dwight Twilley, as well as the Dunn half of country music's superstars, Brooks and Dunn. Although from Texas, Ronnie Dunn came to Tulsa for a chance at the music scene marshalled by industry impresario, Jim Halsey. Dunn found work and inspiration in the country music night club, City Limits, where line dancing sparked their first major hit, "Boot Scootin' Boogie." The duo continued massive success in 2004 with their highly successful *Neon Circus and Wild West Show*. Ronnie Dunn was inducted into the Oklahoma Music Hall of Fame in 2003.

Compared to previous decades, the 1980s proved to be quiet ones in Tulsa, with many major musicians having moved on. However, the return of Steve Ripley to Tulsa in 1986 proved to be a harbinger of better times. Within two years, Ripley recorded and released his first single by The Tractors. By 1994, the first Tractors album, with its persistent nods to both the Tulsa Sound and country music's heritage, became the best-selling country music album in 1994.

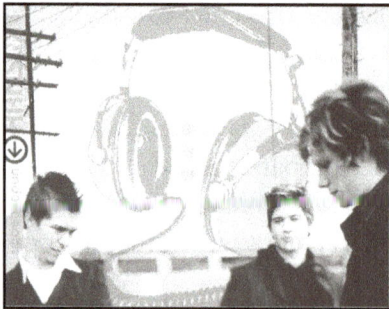

The next successful artists to emerge from Tulsa were another brother act. In 1997, Hanson topped the pop world with their single "MMMbop" from *Middle of Nowhere*. The group continues to tour and record, with their most recent CD, *Underneath* (pictured above), being produced independently by the band in 2004.

Unsurprisingly, the list of Tulsans who are enjoying musical success at the beginning of the twenty-first century is not a short one. While also remembered in Oklahoma as a legendary basketball player, Wayman Tisdale is one of the nation's top contemporary jazz artists. His 2001 CD, *Face to Face*, hit #1 on *Billboard*'s jazz chart, and he was noted as the 2002 Bassist of the Year by the Smooth Jazz Awards. Also in 2002, Oklahoma governor Brad Henry appointed Tisdale to serve on the state tourism and recreation commission.

Also on the contemporary jazz front is Jacob Fred Jazz

Odyssey (JFJO), a well-journeyed group led by keyboardist Brian Haas (left) and bassist Reed Mathis who work with any number of different percussionists and horn players, as well as country and classical musicians. Both musicians received the bulk of the their formal training in Tulsa, and have since released a series of critically acclaimed CDs, performed to ecstatic reviews around the country, and may be the most progressive live jazz combo in America today.

If Route 66 travelers need extended jams to listen to while rolling through the big spaces out West, or increasingly frenetic, but beautifully played, uptempo jazz for rolling back East, the *Oklahoma Music Guide* recommends picking up just about any CDs available featuring this group. For starters, try *All Is One - Live in New York City* (Knitting Factory, 2002). Usually, the group also sells unique or limited edition CDs at their shows, which is where one gets the ultimate appreciation for Jacob Fred Jazz Odyssey's technical abilities, artistic ethos, and interpretive skills.

Listing all of the Tulsa musicians who have made, or are making important, or at least well-liked, music would turn this small publication into a lengthy treatise on only one city. Hot R&B diva Toni Estes, newcoming poprocker Tony Romanello, jazz pianist Mike Leland, and one of the best guitar players in the world, Tommy Crook, all call Tulsa home, and play here regularly. If nothing else, jazz fans, guitar fans, and just fans of music in general should track down guitarist Tommy Crook. He wows 'em very Friday night at Lanna Thai Restaurant on 7227 S. Memorial Boulevard in Tulsa. Call ahead to be sure: (918) 249-5262.

To break into Tulsa's music scene, pick up the *Tulsa World*'s *Spot Magazine* in the Friday paper, or find the free *Urban Tulsa* at various locations around the city. Both have extensive listings of current live music around town, as well as regular features on local and national musicians.

Historic Sites with a Musical Focus

Cain's Ballroom - 423 N. Main (918) 584-2309
Oklahoma Jazz Hall of Fame - Greenwood Cultural Center
 Photos and history of jazz musicians who have made
 contributions to Oklahoma's great jazz legacy, as well as history
 of Tulsa's Greenwood District, also known as "The Black Wall
 Street" in American history. Much of Tulsa's jazz and R&B can
 be traced to the area around Greenwood, Archer, and Pine.

For Vinyl Collectors

•Frontier Records and Tapes 4904-A South Union, Tulsa
•Blue Moon Discs, 3807-C S. Peoria Avenue, Tulsa
•CD Exchange Sounds, 3202 E. 11th Street, Tulsa
•Rob's Records and CDs, 1511 S. Memorial, Tulsa
•Starship Records and Tapes, 2813 E. 11th Street, Tulsa
•Goodwill on Southwest Blvd. Rt. 66, West Tulsa

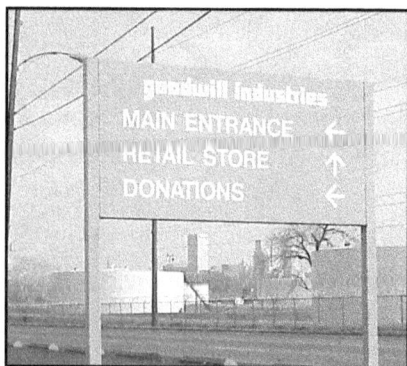

Music Stores

While several
good, and in the
case of Roy and
Candy's, historic,
music stores exist
in Tulsa (consult
any phone book)
Firey Brothers
Music and Pro Audio is the only music store on the original
Route 66 in Tulsa. Find them at 4718 E. 11th, or call (918)
838-9895.

Live Music Venues

See previsoulsy mentioned publications, or
www.tulsamusicscene.com for listings of the multitude of sacred
and secular performance spaces in Tulsa. While stalwarts like
the Tulsa Performing Arts Center, the Brady Theater, and
Cain's Ballroom anchor the downtown entertainment district,
the city has many nightclubs, churches, and university and other
school facilities that present live music regularly. For the Route
66 Flavor, visit Ed's Hurricane Lounge at 3216 E. 11th Street,
or the Stage Door at 10117 E. 11th.

Musical Side Trips

Bartlesville - Held each year in mid-June, the OK Mozart
Festival is a tremendous opportunity to hear some of the
world's finest musicians play in one the most acoustically perfect
performance spaces anywhere, the Bartlesville Community
Center, designed by the Frank Lloyd Wright Foundation. Call
(918) 336-900, or see www.okmozart.com.

Muskogee - Oklahoma Music Hall of Fame, offices open
Monday through Friday, 10 a.m to 4:30 p.m. Check website
for special events at www.oklahomamusichalloffame.com, or
call (918) 687-0800. Live concerts through the summer.

Annual Musical Events in Tulsa

Oklahoma Blues Festival, May, www.okblues.com

Tulsa International Mayfest, May, www.tulsamayfest.com

Light Opera Oklahoma Festival, June, www.lightoperaok.com

Juneteenth Greenwood Festival, June, www.okjazz.org

Powwow of Champions (IICOT), August, (918) 744-1113
  Expo Square, www.iicot.org

Greek Festival, September, Holy Trinity Greek Orthodox
  Church, 1222 S. Guthrie, (918) 583-2082

Oklahoma Scottish Games and Gathering, September,
  Chandler Park, 6500 W. 21st Street, (918) 499-2585
  www.tulsascottishgames.com

Fiesta Tulsa, September, Plaza Santa Cecelia,
  2160 Garnett Road, (918) 664-5236

Festival Espano, September, 3rd and Boulder, (918) 622-8258

Tulsa State Fair, First of October, Expo Square
  www.tulsastatefair.com

Shalomfest, October, Temple Israel, 2004 E. 22nd Place

Oktoberfest, River West Festival Park, (918) 744-9700
  www.tulsaoktoberfest.org

For More Information

If travelers are coming into Tulsa from the east, or leaving
Tulsa from the west, they should try and stop by the Oklahoma
Information Center on I-44 between Catoosa and Tulsa north
of I-44 at Exit 161. Call (918) 439-3212 with questions.

Tulsa Metro Chamber and Visitors Bureau, (918) 585-1201
  (800) 558-3311, www.VisitTulsa.com
  www.tulsachamber.com, www.cityoftulsa.com

Greenwood Chamber of Commerce, (918) 585-2084

Near Sapulpa, looking east to Tulsa from where Interstate 44 and Route 66 converge, or diverge, depending on which way you are going.

Sapulpa

Settled: 1850 by Jim Sapulpa
2000 Population: 19,166

Notable Music History

Lead alto sax player and music director of the Count Basie Orchestra for twenty years (1951-1970), Marshal Royal was born into a musical family in Sapulpa, May 12, 1912. Although more research needs to be done into their Sapulpa background, we know Royal's father was a bandleader, music teacher, and played all the reeds, strings, and some of the valve instruments, while his mother was a piano teacher. Since the family moved to Los Angeles in 1916, Oklahoma ceased to be a factor in Royal's life; however, his parents apparently were part of a significant music society in Sapulpa from at least 1912 to 1914. Often compared to Benny Carter, Royal's rich alto sax solos with a string of excellent big bands made him popular both nationally and internationally. Marshal Royal died in Los Angeles on May 9, 1995. *Marshal Royal: Jazz Survivor*, an autobiography was released in 2001, by Continuum Press.

Historic Sites with a Musical Focus

Sapulpa Historical Museum, 100 E. Lee, (918) 224-4871
   1890s music room, telephone exhibit, railroad memorabilia

Live Music Venue

One spot with live music in Sapulpa is the Hickory House (pictured above). Hear classic country and some 50s rock Thursday and Saturday nights at 626 N. Mission.

Music Store

Like many smaller towns along Oklahoma Route 66, the local pawn shop is often the best place to hunt for musical instruments, CDs, tapes, and other associated materials that hungry, bored, or destitute musicians pawn off occasionally to pay a bill, have a meal, or get a refreshment. In Sapulpa, the very visible Apache Pawn (pictured at right) fills several of those roles at 309 N. Mission.

Annual Musical Events in Sapulpa

Route 66 Blowout, first weekend of June, downtown
  (918) 224-5709, www.sapulpamainstreet.com
Marshal Royal Jazz Festival, July, citywide jazz concerts
  (918) 227-5151, www.sapulpaparks.org

For more Information

Sapulpa Chamber of Commerce, 101 E. Dewey, 74066
  (918) 224-0170
Sapulpa Main Street, 101 E. Dewey, 74066, (918)224-5709

Kellyville

Established: 1893
2000 Population: 906
Notable Music History

While also known as the home of Western Swing Hall of Fame pianist, Clarence Boyd, the Kellyville area is also home to many Euchee people who continue their annual ceremonies

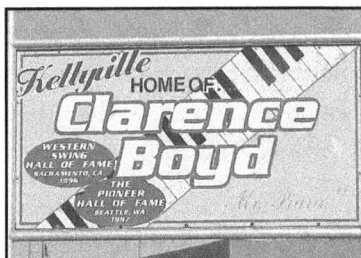

at grounds not far from Kellyville. While part of the Muscogee (Creek) Nation politically, the Euchee have always maintained a distinctive language and set of lifeways. Travelers might notice the Euchee offices on the west side of Sapulpa, or see the Kellyville Indian Community Center just east of Kellyville. Formerly known as the Diamond Ballroom, the building serves as a meeting place and winter activity center for area tribal people. Occasionally, one can stop by and see a flyer for some future activity taped to the inside of the glass doors.

Vinyl Collectors

Stop in the Old Cotton Gin antique shop, flea market, and restaurant (pictured right) to see what's cooking or check out the shelves and see

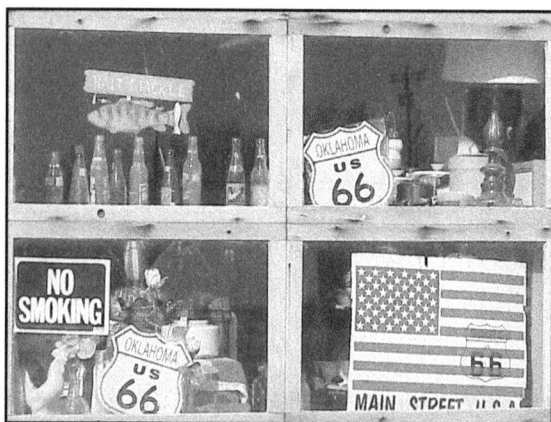

what records have floated into the building lately. Since the Kellyville area is fairly mixed with Anglo/African/American Indian people, record choices tend to be more multi-genre and multi-ethnic than is common for flea market collections for sale.

Annual Musical Events

Euchee Tribe's Green Corn Ceremonial Cycle
  Euchee Tribe, P.O. Box 10, Sapulpa, OK, 74067
  (918)-224-3065

For More Information

Kellyville City Hall (918) 247-6160

Bristow

Established: Founded in 1897 as Woodland Queen of the Creek Nation, founders named the town for its postmaster in 1898.

2000 Population: 4,325

Notable Music History

Emerging in the 1960s as one of the most talented folksingers of the protest era, singer, songwriter, guitarist Tom Paxton (at left) was born on the south side of Chicago, Illinois, but raised in Bristow, where he graduated from high school. His aunt gave him a guitar at age sixteen; and, when Tom entered the University of Oklahoma, he began working up his own repertoire of folk songs, which totaled more than 200 by the time he graduated. First-time listeners will want to track down *I Can't Help Wonder Where I'm Bound: The Elektra Years* (Rhino, 1999), which collects many of his best-known songs. Paxton's recent honors include a 2004 Grammy nomination in the category of Best Musical Album for Children for his CD *Your Shoes My Shoes* (Red House).

Another Bristow native, Tom Skinner (pictured right), is often thought of as a godfather of red dirt music. Tom's story laden songs are available through Binky Records, and his brothers, Mike (fiddle) and Craig (guitar), are also known as excellent musicians.

Finally, Joe Lee Wilson, one of the most popular jazz vocal stylists of the 1970s, was born on a farm near Bristow, Dec. 22, 1935.

Historic Sites with a Musical Focus

Bristow Historical Museum, inside Railroad Depot, 1/2 block east of Main Street, 918-367-5151, Open M-F, Free

For Vinyl Collectors

Bristow has several antique stores. (The Treasure Hunt on Main Street is pictured at right). Travelers who collect records will often find interesting vinyl in these stores at very reasonable prices.

Live Music Venues

Live music oppotunities in Bristow are limited to occasional performances at the amphitheater near the historical museum, and at the Jubilee Center, primarily a Christian life center for young people, but also a center for occasional contemporary Christion rock and pop bands, as well as the monthly gospel sing. Open T, Th, F, Sat. 3:30 pm to 8pm.

Annual Music Events

Gospel Jubilee, 1st Saturday of the month, from 7 p.m. to 9 p.m.
   Jubilee Center, 310 N. Main Street, (918) 367-3053
Western Heritage Days, 2nd weekend in August.
Christmas Parade, 1st Thursday in December.

For More Information

104.9 FM KREK, Local Country Music Radio Station
Bristow Chamber of Commerce, (918) 367-5151
   www.bristowok.org

Musical Side Trip

Bristow is the perfect turn-off point to visit the hometown of Woody Guthrie, Okemah, which is about 31 miles south of Bristow on State Highway 48. Visitors can see the statue of Woody Guthrie in the middle of town (above), or plan on visiting the Woody Guthrie Free Folk Festival, the second weekend of July each year (www.woodyguthrie.com).

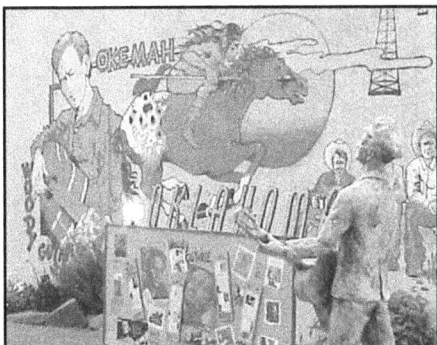

Depew

Established: 1893
2000 Population: 564

Music Venues

Aside from area churches, Buddy's Bar at 415 S. Main Street is the best opportunity to find out about Depew's secular musical aesthetic.

.

For More Information

Depew City Hall
  (918) 324-5251

Leaving Depew, lots of old road ghosts sit north of the highway. Once people cross into Lincoln County, they have passed the old Oklahoma Territory border and are within the current Sac and Fox Nation.

Sac and Fox Nation

Brief Tribal History

While the modern history of the Sac and Fox Nation begins with their arrival in Indian Territory in 1869, the oral history places them at the Saint Lawrence Seaway at the time of first European contact in the 1600s. Subsequently, the Sac and Fox endured the all-too-familiar warfare, treaties, removals, reservations, and, ultimately, allotment of tribal lands to tribal members. Once allotted, the rest could be opened up for settlement in the now famous Oklahoma land runs. Contemporarily, the Sac and Fox Nation maintains its headquarters, library, community building, and powwow grounds about 5 miles south of Stroud on State Highway 99.

Sac and Fox People in Oklahoma, early 1900s

Tribal Music Traditions

While still maintaining their traditional "Drum Dance," the Sac and Fox people may be the most active intertribal powwow hosts in the state. They host the Annual Sac and Fox Powwow on the second weekend of July, which is free and open to the public at the tribe's powwow grounds. Dancers and singers come from around the U.S. to what is simply known as "Stroud Powwow" in the jargon of those who spend every weekend from Memorial Day to Labor on the competition powwow trail. The event is part homecoming, part fair, and part junk food buffet, as well as a spectacular music experience.

Intertribal powwow groups featuring Sac and Fox singers have made several recordings. Rose Hill, essentially a Sac and Fox southern-style powwow group, recorded for Indian House Records in 1995. Singing with leader Lloyd Gwen at that time were singers Donnie Hamilton, and his two sons, Curtis and Juaquin Hamilton-Young Bird. Curtis has become the leader of one of the dominant southern style groups traveling the contemporary national powwow circuit, Young Bird (pictured above with Curtis in the front row wearing the white windbreaker). While the group has several releases on the Canyon label, Young Bird's 2001 release *Change of Life* received a GRAMMY nomination for Best Native American Recording that year. As much jazz, blues, gospel, country, rock, or classical CDs that travelers bring along for the ride, no collection is complete without some Oklahoma powwow music, and Young Bird is a good place to begin.

Another singer with Sac and Fox heritage, as well as Otoe and Ioway ancestors, is Billy McClellan, Sr., who has recorded two discs of peyote music that is usually associated with the Native American Church. See www.coolrunningsmusic.com.

Almost any weekend of the year one can find a dance going on at the Sac and Fox Nation Community Building. Powwows are held as fundraisers for area school programs and the annual powwow fund, and as honor dances for elders, veterans, and graduates, as well as celebrations for Valentine's Day, anniversaries, and other special occasions.

Powwows in Oklahoma, especially the ones held by the Sac and Fox Nation, are always free and open to the public. Visitors are only expected to act with respect, refrain from any alcohol use before or during the powwow, and ask before taking a photograph or video of someone or a dance. The always-present emcee is a dependable point of contact to ask a question about etiquette. The events are extremely family friendly, and people of all ages bring their lawn chairs to enjoy hours of good singing, dancing, fellowship, and food.

Annual Music Events

Annual Sac and Fox Nation Powwow, 2nd weekend in June
  Sac and Fox Nation Powwow Grounds, 5 1/2 miles south of
  Stroud on Highway 99.

For More Information

Sac and Fox Nation, Route 2, Box 246, Stroud, OK 74071
  (918) 968-3526 or www.cowboy.net/native/sacnfox.html

Local Radio Station in This Area

KUSH from Cushing is an interesting independent Americana radio station at 1600 AM. Featuring traditional, contemporary, and alternative country during the week, the station also airs a locally-produced, American Indian community-oriented radio program. Native Air is broadcast Saturday mornings from 10:00 a.m. to 11:00 a.m. The regular broadcast hours for KUSH are generally from sunrise to sunset. (918) 225-0922

Stroud

Established as a trading post since the 1890s.

2000 Population: 2,758

Notable Music History

With the distinction of being two miles inside of "wet" Oklahoma Territory of the 1890s, as opposed to "dry" Indian Territory, Stroud had at least nine flourishing saloons at the time of statehood in 1907. One can only imagine the honky tonk or barrelhouse piano that must have been played there, a la Scott Joplin who is known to have traveled the territories. Stroud was a border town by today's standards, and adventurers will notice a little of that frontier attitude still in the town's diners and bars, such as the Cue and Brew that is dimly lit, casually comfortable, and has a good jukebox.

For Vinyl Collectors

Periodically, the Antique Mall on Main Street will surprise you.

Music Store

Still don't have the 1-4-5 down? Check Parker's Pawn Shop at the intersection of Route 66 and Highway 99 for a reasonably priced guitar, or pick up some road music from the CD rack, or vintage collection of used cassettes.

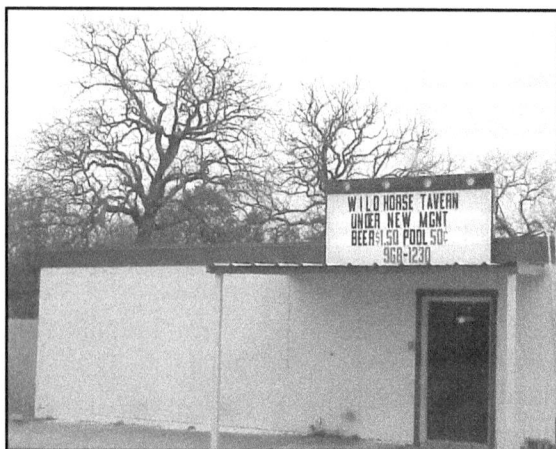

Live Music Venue

The Wild Horse Tavern, west of Stroud on Route 66, alternates between live bands and karaoke on weekends.

For More Information about Stroud

Stroud Chamber of Commerce
216 W. Main
(918) 968-3321
www.stroudok.com

Davenport

Established: 1890
2000 Population: 881
Music Notability:
  Davenport's primary music is in the town's churches. As of 2004, musically-inclined citizens planned on raising local support to increase city sales taxes in order to start a school band program.

Annual Music Events

Nettie Davenport Day, May, (918) 377-2241
Route 66 Car Show, Sept. (918) 377-2241

For More Information
Davenport Chamber of Commerce
ww.davenportok.org

Chandler

Established: 1891
2000 Population: 2,842
Notable Music History
  Not only is Chandler the birthplace of Roy Harris, one of the most important figures in the establishment of twentieth century American symphonic music, the town has also produced the Gillian Family, noted for excellent, stringed instrument work in the country music field.

Roy Harris   Classical composer
Born: February 12, 1898, in Chandler
Died: October 1, 197,9 in Santa Monica, California
Notability: Born in a log cabin on land where the family settled via one of the land runs of the 1890s, Roy Harris did not spend a long time in Chandler. According to Harris's biographer, Dan Stehman, "harsh frontier living conditions" compounded the respiratory problems Roy's mother endured. His father, "bolstered by a gambling win," according to Stehman, sold the "already mortgaged property' and returned to southern California in 1903, when Roy was only five. According to Stehman, Harris learned music from his parents who would sing "folksongs" and accompany themselves with guitar. After also learning the rudiments of piano as a youngster from his mother, Roy began taking lessons, and the rest is American music history. Before his death, several tibutes were established for Harris, including the Roy Harris Archive at California State University-Los Angeles (1973), and the Roy Harris Society (1979). The latter organization was formed to promote performances, recordings, and research dealing with Roy's career.

Historic Site of Significance in Chandler

To get a feel for Pioneer history in Oklahoma Territory, and see a miniature violin made from the dook of Abraham Lincoln, visit to the Lincoln County Historical Museum.
M-F 9:30am to 4 pm
(405)258-2999

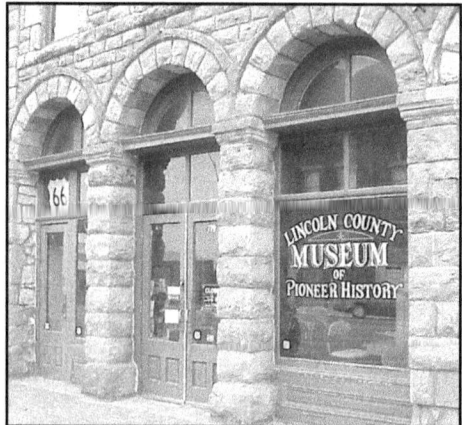

Music Store in Chandler

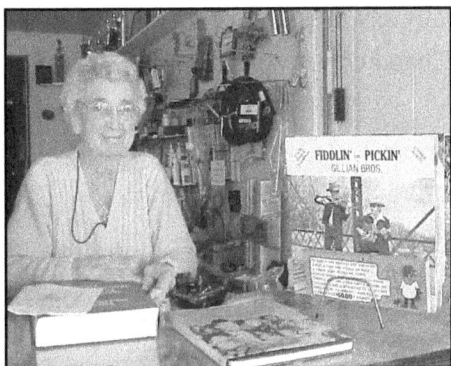

Leota Gillian, mother of Chandler natives Steve and Russ Gillian, both of whom are grand national champions on fiddle and guitar respectively, will open the door to Gillian Music just west of Chandler on Route 66, if you knock on the door of the house next to the store. Vinyl collectors will take note of the Gillian Brothers album *Fiddlin'- Pickin'*, for sale on the counter. Also in the family are Chandler natives Joe Gillian, who has played bass for Ty England, and Amy Gillian, a drummer and lawyer who now works for Sony-Nashville.

Live Music Venues

When traveling through Oklahoma, music fans will notice a number of buildings that look like taverns, but have a sign that indicates some sort of privateness, like "Elks Lodge" or "VFW." Organizations vary from town to town, but VFW (Veterans of Foreign Wars) Post 1719, just west of Chandler about a block north of Route 66 (watch for a sign), has karaoke every weekend and is open to the public. For adventurers who want an authentic, middle-of-Oklahoma, and, therefore, middle of the U.S., perspective of life from some salty veterans and their friends, this is the place.

Musical Side Trips

Sparks America Biker Rally, last weekend of June.
Highway 18B, South of Chandler, www.sparksamerica.com

For More Information

Chandler Chamber of Commerce, 804 Manvel Ave, 7834
 (405) 258-0673 www.chandlerok.com
Stehman, Dan. *Roy Harris: A Bio-Bibliography*. Westport,
   CT: Greenwood Press, 1991. ISBN 0-313-25079-0

Warwick

Established: 1892   *2000 Population:* 235

For Vinyl Collectors

Visit the Seaba Engine Rebuilding garage to pick up antiques, Route 66 memorabilia, and an evolving collection of 78 and 33 rpm vinyl.

For More Information

Town Hall
(405) 258-4090

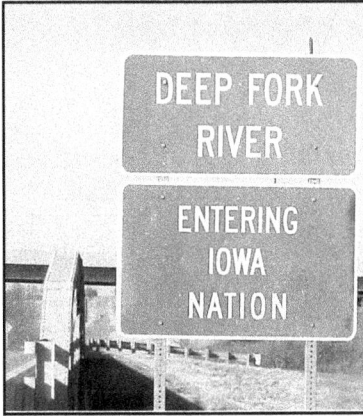

Musical Side Trips

Less than one mile west of Warwick's Seaba Station, Route 66 intersects with U.S. 177. By turning north and crossing the Deep Fork River, travelers will be journeying in the Iowa Nation. On the third weekend of June each year, the tribe hosts an intertribal powwow that is free and open to the public.

The powwow grounds are only about 15 miles north of Route 66. If inclimate weather occurs, the powwow is moved indoors to a building for just such a purpose. The all-weekend event follows the

basic protocol of many Oklahoma powwows, with gourd dancing each day before the intertribal dance, youth contest dancing on Friday nights, adult women contest dancing on Saturday night, and adult men contest dancing on Sunday night.

Eddie and Anthony Arkeketa
(right to left)
of the Redland Singers
at the 2003 Iowa Powwow.

For More Information
Iowa Tribe of Oklahoma
(405) 547-5294

Kickapoo Tribe of Oklahoma

Brief Tribal History

Traditionally from the Great Lakes region, specifically southern Wisconsin at the time of first European contact, the Kickapoo migrated through southern Illinois after the French and Indian War, signing their first treaty with the U.S. in 1795. In 1819, the tribe ceded all of its land in Illinois for land in Missouri, at which point part of the tribe moved to Texas, and then on to Mexico. In 1835, the tribe signed another treaty relinquishing their lands in Missouri for a reservation in northeast Kansas. Kansas began gobbling that land up, allotting parcels to Kickapoos who wished to become Kansas citizens, and the rest of the tribal members moved on to Indian Territory in 1883. After the several moves, it should come as no surprise that two-thirds of the tribe refused to acknowledge the ceding of land back to the U.S. in 1891, but the people had to either take the allotments or nothing. In 1895, the Kickapoo Reservation was included as part of Oklahoma Territory, and lands that had not been allotted to tribal members were open to non-Kickapoo settlement. Route 66 goes just through the northern edge of the current Kickapoo Tribe of Oklahoma's jurisdiction. Travelers would turn south on State Highway 102 for about 11 miles to visit the tribal complex.

Annual Music Events

Started in 1976, the Annual Kickapoo Powwow usually takes place in mid-August. Contact the tribal headquarters to confirm dates. Kickapoo flyers routinely exclaim, "Everyone is welcome!" A Friday and Saturday affair with intertribal dancing well into both nights (usually no contests), the event is held at the Kickapoo Tribal Grounds, 2 miles north of McCloud, Oklahoma, on Highway 102. For specific dates, contact the tribal office.

For More Information

Kickapoo Tribe of Oklahoma
  P.O. Box 70, McCloud, OK 74581 (405) 964-2075

Wellston

Established in 1880, as a trading post on the Kickapoo Reservation; as a result was the first Anglo settlement in Lincoln County.

2000 Population: 825

Notable Music History

Norma Jean   Country singer

Born: January 30, 1948, in a farmhouse near Wellston

Notability: Best remembered as "Pretty Miss Norma Jean,"

Porter Wagoner's singing partner on his television show from 1960 to 1967, Norma Jean Beasler's family moved to Oklahoma City when she was five. From 1963 to 1973, Norma Jean recorded twenty-seven albums for RCA Victor, with hits such as "Let's Go All the Way," "I Wouldn't Buy a Used Car from Him," and "I'm a Walkin' Advertisement for the Blues."

Musical Side Trips

Tourists interested in Oklahoma college town life can drive thirty miles north on 177 and visit Stillwater, Oklahoma, home of Oklahoma State University. Musical highlights include "The Strip," with several clubs featuring live music on Thursdays, Fridays, and Saturdays. Visit Willie's Saloon, where Garth Brooks started out, or the Tumbleweed Dance Hall west of town. Count on country and rock every weekend, and occasional jazz, reggae, and blues acts, with classical music performances seasonally at OSU's Seretean Center. Stillwater Visitors Bureau, (800) 991-6717 or www.come2stillwater.com

For More Information

City of Wellston (405) 356-2476

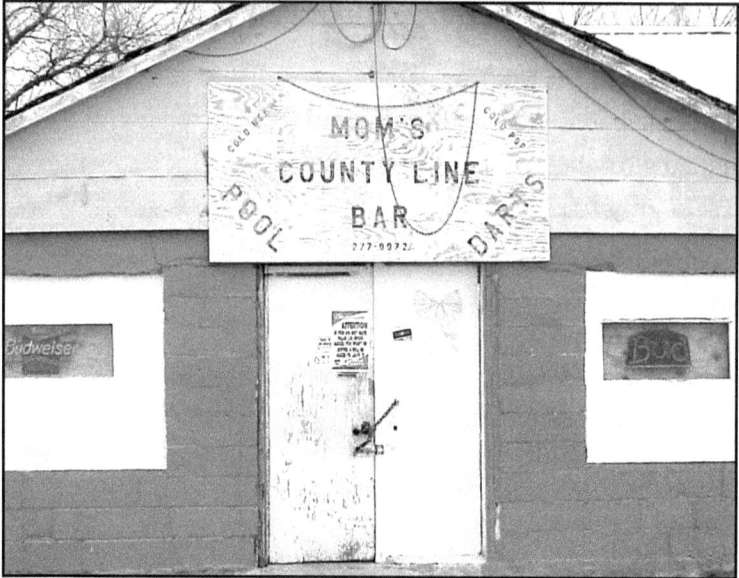

Just inside the eastern edge of Oklahoma County on Route 66 is Mom's County Line Bar, where karaoke singing is a regular weekend activity. Nobody cares if you are out of tune, so go on.

Luther

Established: 1898, as a Frisco Railroad Station
2000 Population: 612

Occasional Live Music
Tres Suenos (Three Dreams) Winery,
19691 E. Charter Oak Road,
Special Events, Wine Tasting, Tours
(405) 277-7089

For More Information
Luther Town Hall, 1919 S. Main, (405) 3833

Arcadia

Established: 1889   *2000 Population:* 279

Live Music Venues
Hillbillee's Cafe, Bed and Breakfast
208 E. Hwy 66, Arcadia, (405) 396-2982
www.hillbillees.com

Notable Music History
Jazz bandleader Al Dennie was born in Arcadia in 1903.

Historic Sites with a Musical Focus
Arcadia's Round Barn (pictured above) has been used many
times over the years for dances. Open Tues. through Sunday,
10a.m. to 5p.m. Free admission. (405) 396-2761

For More Information
Arcadia Town Hall (405) 396-2899

Edmond

Established in 1889 land run, but a settlement since 1887.
2000 Population: 68,315

Notable Music History

While the University of Central Oklahoma and its music program is the center of Edmond's music scene, the city is also the birthplace of Mikaila, a pop singer who has toured as an opening act for Britney Spears, performed at Carnegie Hall, landed a pop single, "So in Love With Two," on the charts in 2001, and has appeared on PBS, Fox-TV, Nickelodeon, and MTV.

University of Central Oklahoma

The first institution of higher learning in Oklahoma Territory, UCO began as the Territorial Normal School in 1890, the first purpose of which was to educate teachers. With 14,000 students enrolled today in five undergraduate colleges, the university's College of Arts, Media, and Design contains the multi-faceted music program that presents more than 200 performing and visual arts events each year, which are all open to the public.

Each year, the UCO School of Music and Department of Theatre, Dance and Media Arts showcases its award-wining talents in a packed performing arts season, to include two musicals, two operas, four theatre productions, two dance concerts, and hosts several additional music peformances from the school's various ensembles.

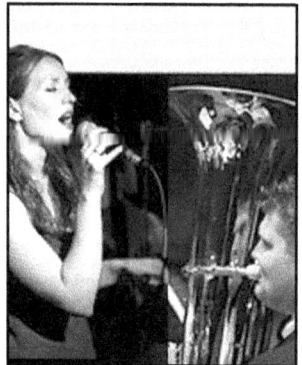

The UCO Jazz Lab (right), the school's live music club, showcases the region's top jazz and blues performers every Thursday, Friday, and Saturday nights. Doors open at 6 p.m., and all shows are $7.00, unless otherwise indicated. The Jazz Lab also hosts several headliner concerts throughout the year. For more information, call (405) 359-7989, visit at 100 E. 5th Street in Edmond, or see www.ucojazzlab.com.

Mitchell Hall (left), dedicated in 1926, has a rich history of famous personalities, as well as legions of student performers, who have graced its stage: comedian W.C. Fields, aviator Amelia Earhart, poet Robert Frost, author James Dickey, big band leader Stan Kenton, jazz legend Clark Terry, and concert pianist Valery Kuleshov. The university's Broadway Tonight series has hosted national tours of Broadway musicals and concerts featuring Oklahomans Patti Page and Sandi Patti, as well as The Lettermen, Shirley Jones, and pianist Roger Williams. For ticket and schedule info: (405) 974-3374

Historic Sites with a Musical Focus

With some antique pianos and photographs of musicians and bands, the Edmond Historical Society Museum does have some information regarding the history of music in the city. Visit the museum at 431 S. Boulevard, Edmond, OK 73034, call (405) 348-0078, or see www.edmondhistory.org

Music Store

Edmond Music
3400 Broadway
Edmond, OK 73013
(405) 348-0004
Great guitar selection, and a piano room with many top-end brands of pianos on display.

Annual Musical Events

The Central Oklahoma Concert Series
  Sponsored by the Chopin Society of Mid-America
  Call (405) 340-3500 or visit www.chopinsociety.com
Strawhat Musical Theatre, and Summer Ice Cream and
  Watermelon Band Festivals, on the front lawn of Mitchell Hall.
Downtown Arts Festival, 2nd weekend in May, Live Music.
Edmond Blues and Jazz Festival, May, (405) 341-3321.
Concerts in the Park, Hafer Park, 9th and Bryant, Free.
  June through August. (405) 359-4630

For More Information

Edmond Convention and Visitors Bureau
  825 E. 2nd Street, Suite 100, Edmond, 73012
  (405) 341-4344 or www.visitedmondok.com

Musical Side Trip

Only twelve miles north of Edmond, Guthrie has a beautiful Victorian downtown, befitting the town's status as the first capitol of Oklahoma. Multiple antique stores make the city a treasure trove of 78s, old phonograph players, and vintage musical instruments. In addition, Guthrie is also home to the Double Stop Fiddle Shop and Music Hall, owned and operated by Byron Berline (pictured above). Along with the fiddle shop, Berline also runs the Double Stop Music Hall right upstairs from the fiddle shop. Performances occur about every two weeks, on the weekends, with Byron's band performing sometimes, and other groups coming in to play at other times.

A three-time world fiddle champion who has performed with the Rolling Stones, The Byrds, The Eagles, Elton John and Bob Dylan, as well as with Bill Monroe and Oklahoma native Vince Gill, Berline is also the brains behind the Oklahoma International Bluegrass Festival, usually held in early October in Guthrie. The event has become one the nation's premier bluegrass festivals, bringing in major headliners like Sam Bush each year, as well providing a forum for international, local, and youth bluegrass groups. Call (405) 282-6646 for the Fiddle Shop or Music Hall. Call (405) 282-4446 or see www.oibf.com for the festival.

Guthrie is also home to the National Four-String Banjo Hall of Fame Museum, the only museum of its kind in America. The museum is free, but donations are encouraged. Call the museum at (405) 260-1323 or visit www.banjomuseum.org. To hear the live banjo playing, Memorial Day Weekend is the time for the annual Jazz Banjo Festival. Call (800) OK BANJO for more information, or see www.banjofestival.com.

Oklahoma City

Established April 22, 1889, when the unassigned Oklahoma Territory was opened to non-Indian settledment.

2000 Population: 506,132

Notable Music History

Like any state capitol, Oklahoma City has benefitted culturally, economically, and population-wise from being the center of the state's government, and the center of the state as a whole. Oklahoma City is the crossroads of the state, and some maintain it's even the crossroads of this part of the U. S. As a result, many people of many different backgrounds have come through Oklahoma City, including several musicians. To document the entire city's musical legacy is better left to a long-form work like the *Oklahoma Music Guide*. However, just mentioning the musicians who have come from the city to enjoy success on a national scale will take some time in itself.

From 1900 to 1945, forty-eight jazz musicians of national significance were born in the state of Oklahoma. Of that number, eleven were born in Oklahoma City: trumpeter Buddy Anderson (b. 1919) who played with Charlie Christian and Jay McShann; bassist Abe Bolar (b. 1909) of the Oklahoma City Blue Devils, an outstanding "territory band" that went on to form the nucleus of the first Count Basie Orchestra; saxophonist Henry Bridges (b. 1908); free-jazz trumpeter Don Cherry (b. 1936); trombonist Ted Donnelly (b. 1912) who played with Count Basie (1943-1950) and Erskine Hawkins (1951-1957); and tenor saxophonist Wardell Gray (b. 1921), the "best new tenor sax star of 1948, who played with Charlie Parker, Count Basie, Earl Hines, and Benny Goodman when Goodman began experimenting with bebop. Perhaps the most significant recordings by Gray were made with Dexter Gordon in 1952 for an album on Decca Records, *The Chase*. It is this album, now almost impossible to collect, that features "The Hunt," a song that was inspirational for Jack Kerouac in his own road story, *On the Road*.

Saxophonist/clarinettist/vocalist Lemuel C. Johnson (b. 1909) took up clarinet his junior year at Douglass High Schooll in Oklahoma City. Johnson played with Louis Armstrong and Fats Waller and toured internationally with the Harlem Blues and Jazz Band. Drummer Don LaMond (b. 1920) played with Woody Herman's band for many years and recorded with Bob Crosby, Benny Goodman, Quincy Jones, Stan Getz, and Charlie Parker. Vocalist Marilyn Moore (b. 1931) sang in clubs in Oklahoma City in high school before working in Chicago, and later singing with Woody Herman and Charlie Barnet.

Known as Mr. 5 x 5 because of his short and round stature, Jimmy Rushing (b. 1903) is thought to be one of the great male vocalists in jazz history. Rushing's father played trumpet, his mother played piano and sang in choirs, and his brother was a singer. Rushing left for California in 1923 but returned to Oklahoma City in 1925 where he played with Walter Page and then joined the Blue Devils in 1929. Rushing sang with Bennie

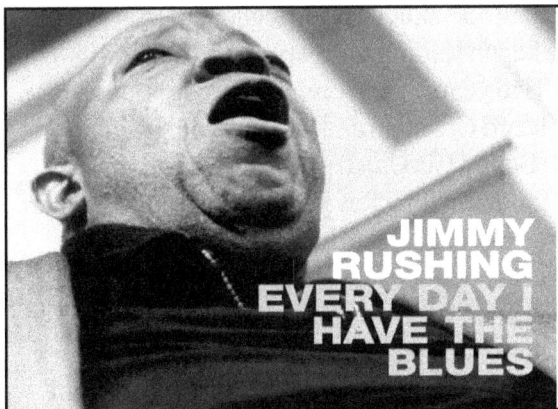

Moten's group out of Kansas City from 1929 to 1935, and then joined Count Basie's group where he stayed until 1950.

Another reason for the development of so many jazz musicians in Oklahoma City was the number of outlets (clubs, cafes, theaters, and ballrooms) that were available for amateur and professional musicians. Second Street, or "Deep Deuce," was the center of Oklahoma City jazz with places like Ruby's Grill, Richardson's Shoe Shine Parlor, and Rushing's Cafe, all catering to jazz music. Out of this environment came the Texas-born, but Oklahoma City-raised, Charlie Christian (pictured left).

The first significant soloist on the electric guitar in any music genre and one of the major role models for all jazz guitarists from 1940 onward, Charles Henry Christian was born in Bonham, Texas, but the family moved to Oklahoma City when "Charlie" was two years old. Starting on trumpet, Christian switched to guitar at about age twelve, making his first guitar out of cigar boxes in manual training class at Douglass High School. After apprenticing in several territory bands, groups usually based in urban centers that served black audiences throughout the Southwest and Midwest, he began leading his own combo in 1937 in Oklahoma City. Two years later Columbia Records talent scout John Hammond heard Christian and took the young guitarist to California to join Benny Goodman's band. After touring and recording with Goodman for a few years, the group wound up in New York City, where Christian became involved in the nascent 52nd Street bebop scene with Dizzy Gillespie, Thelonious Monk, and Oklahoma saxophonist Don Byas. The city proved to be his undoing, however, as by age twenty-five Charlie Christian was dead of tuberculosis, aided by alcohol abuse.

While jazz certainly flourished in Oklahoma City from the early 1900s until World War II, a number of country music artists have also emerged from Oklahoma City, or migrated to

town to enhance their career. Wiley Walker and Gene Sullivan, although born in Florida and Alabama respectively, teamed up 1939 in Dallas before moving to OKC in 1941. The duo (pictured left) enjoyed wide success as songwriters, with their tunes being recorded by artists such as Jerry Lee Lewis, Leon Russell, Hank Williams, Sr., and Elvis Presley, all of whom had a hit with Wiley and Gene's "When My Blue Moon Turns to Gold Again."

In the late 1940s, Wiley and Gene entered the new medium of television, and for several years hosted the *Oklahoma Jamboree* on KOCO-TV in Oklahoma City. The duo faded from the national music scene in the 1960s, but Gene Sullivan operated a studio in Oklahoma City where many of the Tulsa Sound musicians came to record, and in the 1970s ran a music store.

Several other country musicians were born in Oklahoma City: yodeler Molly Bee (b. 1939); ultimate steel guitarist Noel Boggs (b. 1917); Henson Cargill (b. 1941), known for his 1968 #1 hit "Skip a Rope," but also for his hilarious "Oklahoma Hell," a 1972 tale about the singer's father who discovers oil on the parched family farmland. After the father is redeemed by prayer and faith in God's plan, Cargill (at right) sings, "God smiled down from heaven on Dad's Oklahoma Hell."

Additional OKC natives include Nashville Songwriters Hall of Fame member Tommy Collins (b. 1930); outlaw country figure Alvin Crow (b. 1950); modern pop country artist Ty England (b. 1963); Oklahoma State University Rhodes Scholar and Delicious Militia singer/songwriter Blaine Greteman; and Tommy Overstreet (b. 1937), known for "Ramona" and "My Blue Heaven," who saw his star placed on the Country Music Hall of Fame Walkway of Stars in 1985. Additionally, while neither Buck Owens nor Conway Twitty were born in Oklahoma, both spent productive parts of their career in the state. Owens recorded his 1960s syndicated TV program *Buck Owens' Ranch* at WKY in Oklahoma City. Conway Twitty resided in Oklahoma City from the mid-1960s through 1975, basing his tour operations and recording plans from the city during that period.

Composer or co-composer of three huge 1960s hits, "Greenback Dollar," "Green, Green," and "Eve of Destruction," as well as lead singer with the New Christy Minstrels through most of the first half of the 1960s, Barry McGuire (above) was born in the city in 1935. Serendipitously for this book, McGuire was a minor actor on the *Route 66* TV show.

The Flaming Lips (left) are the best-known, and most significant, contemporary Oklahoma rock group, having won a 2003 Grammy Award for Best Rock Instrumental Performance. Formed in 1983, the group's popularity hinges on theatrical shows, creative videos, and optimistic rock that is unapologetic for sensitivity to life's most complex issues, i.e., time, death, love, and fulfillment of individual purpose without compromising one's ideals. Born in Pittsburgh (1965), group leader Wayne Coyne (center) has lived in OKC since he was a small child.

Million-selling Color Me Badd, whose hits in the early 1990s included the #1 "I Adore Mi Amor," formed in 1987 at Northwest Classen High School. By combining tight vocal harmonies with origins in doo-wop and 1960s R & B and thumping bass lines and beats of 1980s hip hop, Color Me Badd was in the thick of a resurgence of pop vocal groups, such as En Vogue and Boyz II Men. The group's catchy, if not saucy, romantic ballads and made-for-video dance moves foretold the "boy band" trend of American popular music in the late 1990s, exemplified by N'Sync and Backstreet Boys.

Significant musicians more associated with Tulsa than OKC where they were born include singer/songwriter/guitarist J.J. Cale (1938) and bassist Carl Radle (b. 1942), one of the most sought after rock and blues bassists of the 1970s, who played with Eric Clapton (on "Layla," among others), John Lee Hooker, Buddy Guy, Duane Allman, Dr. John, Rita Coolidge, and George Harrison on the Concert for Bangladesh. Radle died in 1980.

Musicians from other genres who have emerged from Oklahoma City include Contemporary Christian star Sandi Patty (b. 1957) and newcomer Kristy Starling (b. 1981). NewAge/American Indian producer and composer Jim Wilson, also known as Little Wolf. Jazz guitarist Benny Garcia, Jr. (b. 1926) played with Tex Williams, Johnnie Lee Wills, and Benny Goodman, and still owns the tortoise shell guitar pick Charlie Christian's mother gave the young Garcia when the two became friends after Charlie died. Mike Brewer (b. 1944), half of Brewer Shipley, known for "One Toke Over the Line" is also an OKC native.

Singer/songwriter/mandolinist John Cooper of the Red Dirt Rangers is an Oklahoma City native (b. 1958) and is further connected to this book and the road by the Rangers covering "Used to Be," a Tom Skinner/Bob Wiles composition about a once active and now lonely stretch of Route 66 included on *The Songs of Route 66: Music from the All-American Highway* (Lazy SOB, 1995). Along with Ben Han and Brad Piccolo, Cooper and the Rangers have several albums out that have fallen under the loosely-defined banner of Red Dirt music, which turns up varying degrees of rock, blues, folk, country, and even jazz, depending on the circumstance or audience. While Piccolo and Cooper had played together some in Stillwater at Oklahoma State University in the early 1980s, the duo added Ben Han on lead guitar when they all jammed together in the mid-1980s in Oklahoma City. Named after the color of dirt known as the Central Rolling Red Prairies among soil surveyors, the music has come to represent a modern Oklahoma ethos founded by the wit of Will Rogers, the multi-faceted Wills Western swing bands, and the folkstory singing of Woody Guthrie.

Many more musicians are making headway out of a career in Oklahoma City, where the rent is usually low and the geographic location puts a group or solo performer 5 to 7 hours from several cities with music scenes, such as the major college towns of Texas, or the major regional cities in border states Arkansas, New Mexico, Missouri, Colorado, and Kansas.

While a couple of groups to look out for include The Candles and Starlight Mints, really interested music fans should thoroughly review www.oklahomarock.com for the best info on independent Oklahoma rock groups, as well as extremely detailed sections on OKC venues, live shows, and indie-rock news. For weekly updates on local music, who's who, and who is playing where, see the weekly free paper, *Oklahoma Gazette*, available at coffee shops, bookstores, video stores, and most stores that sell recorded music, or the Friday edition of the *Daily Oklahoman*. Travelers will find virtually every genre of American music being performed in Oklahoma City, especially in the summer months when many festivals feature live entertainment.

Historic Sites with a Musical Focus

A very exciting development for those people interested in the preservation of Oklahoma history, the $50 million Oklahoma History Center (below) is scheduled for opening on statehood day, November 16, 2005. Operated by the Oklahoma Historical Society, the world-class museum is the home for many artifacts relating to the musical traditions of Oklahoma. Focusing on the state's multi-cultural heritage, settlement,

agricultural and economic development, the current museum is still open, still interesting, and still free at 2100 N. Lincoln Avenue, Monday through Saturday from 10 a.m. to 5 p.m. Call (405) 522-5244, or see www.ok-history.mus.ok.us.

Oklahoma City has a multitude of live music venues that can be found quickly through the previously mentioned sources, but travelers wanting OKC's 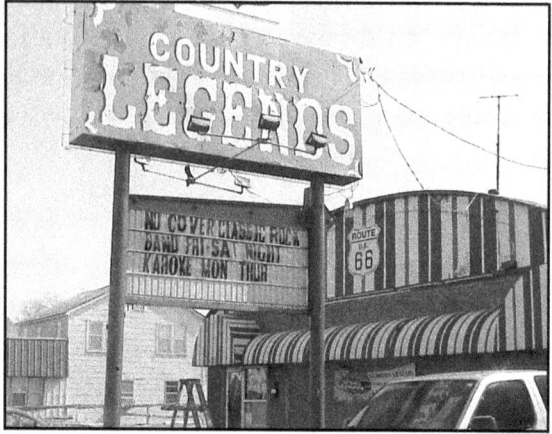 live spots on Route 66 will have to check out the all-ages live music every Saturday afternoon at 66 Bowl, 3810 NW 39th Expressway (Route 66). The over twenty-one types can sit at Country Legends, just west of 66 Bowl at 4328 NW 39th Expressway (Route 66), but don't be fooled by the name. The club features classic rock and blues. Call (405) 946-1751. For insight into Oklahoma City's hometown country music scene, check out the Oklahoma Opry, with live music by local and national country acts, Saturday nights at 404 W. Commerce, or call (888) 801-6495 for more information.

Oklahoma City's Civic Center Music Hall has been beautifully renovated and acoustically improved. The 2004 calendar listed national artists such as Harry Connick, Jr., Broadway touring companies, ballet, and classical music by the Oklahoma City Philharmonic. 201 N. Walker Avenue. Call (405) 297-2584, or see www.okciviccenter.org.

The new Wanda L. Bass Music Center at Oklahoma City University will become a performance space unequaled along Route 66 in Oklahoma, and rarely anywhere.

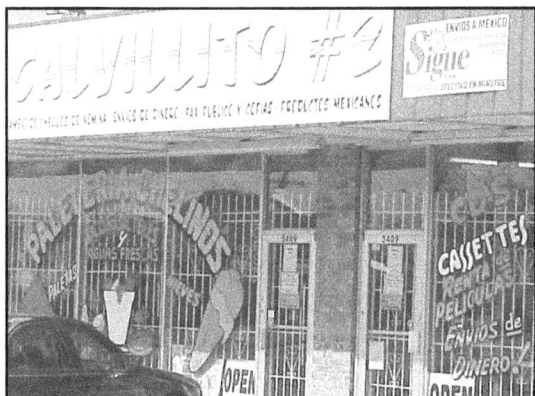

Music Store
West of downtown OKC on Route 66, one can see the ever-shifting demographics of Oklahoma's people, and pick up a Latin CD or cassette.

Annual Musical Events

Festival of the Arts [four stages with non-stop music], April,
  Myriad Botanical Gardens, (405) 270-4848.

Canterbury Choral Festival, Civic Center Music Hall
  May through June, (405) 232-7464.

Paseo Arts Festival [showcases Oklahoma music talent],
  NW Dewey and 30th, (405) 427-2688.

Red Earth American Indian Festival, State Fair Park, June,
  (405) 427-5228 or www.redearth.org.

Sunday Twilight Concerts, June and July, (405) 270-4848,
  Will Rogers Amphitheatre, Myriad Botanical Gardens.

Deep Deuce Jazz Festival, N.E. 2nd and Walnut, October,
  (405) 524-3800.

Good Medicine Society New Year's Sobriety Powwow,
  State Fairgrounds, Kitchens of American Building,
  (405) 943-7935.

For Vinyl Collectors

Music Dimensions, 16th and Meridian NW, (405) 946-4492.

Old Paris Flea Market, 1111 South Eastern,
  Open Saturday and Sunday, 9:00 a.m. to 6 p.m.

One Tribe Records, 2412 NW 23rd Street, (405) 521-8188.

For More Information

Oklahoma City Convention and Visitors Bureau,
  189 W. Sheridan, OKC, OK 73102,
  (800) 225-5652 or www.visitokc.com.
Online live music listings in Oklahoma City,
  see www.okclive.com.
Oklahoma Welcome Center on I-35, just north of Frontier City
  at I-44 interchange (405) 478-4637, travel information.

Musically Related Side Trips

The National Cowboy Hall of Fame, 1700 N.E. 63rd, OKC
  405- 478-2250 or www.cowboyhalloffame.org,
  9 a.m. to 5 p.m. Labor Day to Memorial Day,
  8:30 a.m. to 6 p.m. Memorial Day to Labor Day.
  Singing cowboys are part of the story here.
Oklahoma City National Memorial and Museum
  (405) 235-3313 or 1-888-542-HOPE,
  Outdoor symbolic memorial is open 24/7,
  museum open Monday through Saturday 9:00 a.m to 6 p.m.
   museum open Sunday 1 p.m. to 6 p.m.Ticket sales stop 5 p.m.
  Obviously, this memorial is not included here to be flip;
   however, the site and the event have inspired numerous songs
  and lyrics in songs, from rap to country, so it is included here
  with respect to the awe, fear, and pride it engenders as a
  place in Oklahoman, American, and world memory.
Norman is thirty minutes south of Oklahoma City and is the
  location of the University of Oklahoma and, therefore, has a
  substantial local music scene, both formal via the university,
  and local, independent rock via college-aged kids, and kids
  who just won't grow up. See www.normanmusicscene.com,
Gene Autry Museum - 90 miles south, but an entire museum
  dedicated to movie singing cowboys, (580) 294-3047.
Percussive Arts Society Museum - 90 miles southwest -
  13,000 square foot collection of rare percussive instruments
  from around the world. Hands-on exhibit for kids. Lawton
  701 NW Ferris Ave., (580) 353-1455, or www.pas.org.

Note to Westbound Old Road Followers:

Driving west out of Oklahoma City on 23rd Street, drivers should turn north on May Avenue to get to 39th Street, also known as 39th Expressway, which is the pathway of Historic Route 66. As of spring 2004, if west-bound drivers on 23rd Street see a small, red quarter note on the north side of the street in a front yard, then they have missed the turn at May.

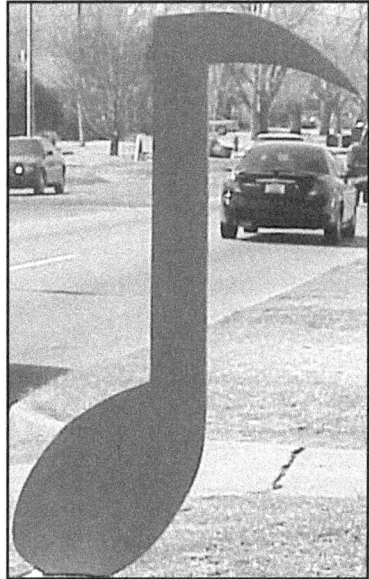

Warr Acres

Established in 1948 as an Oklahoma City suburb.
2000 Population: 9,735
Notable Music History
Aside from area churches, the primary music activity here is in the excellent band progams of the Putnam City Schools.

Music Stores
Not a music store, per se, First Cash Pawn on NW 39th does have some guitars.

For More Information
Warr Acres City Hal
(405) 789-2892

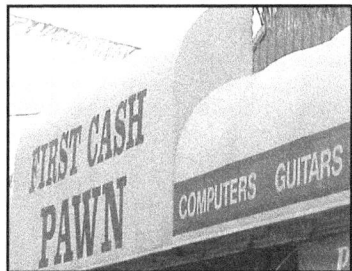

Bethany

Established: 1908

2000 Population: 20, 307

Live Music Venues

Aside from a small theater in the back of A Singing Station, and various churches in town, Southern Nazarene University has the primary performance space in Bethany.

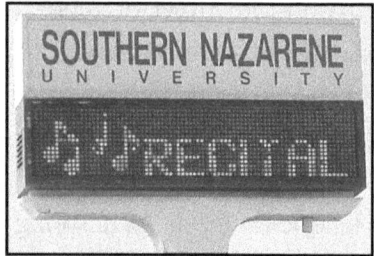

Music Stores

A Singing Station, 6628 NW Expressway (Route 66), or (405) 789-NOTE, sells soundtracks for karaoke, and features a live, free variety show the first Friday of each month. Owner Valerie Strain also teaches vocal music.

David's Music Plus, 6236 NW 39th or (405) 789-2112, carries guitars, amps, accessories, drums, *Oklahoma Gazettes*,and a wall's worth of new and used CDs.

For More Information

Northwest Chamber, 7440 NW 39th, (405) 789-1256.

Yukon

Established in 1891 within seven miles of Oklahoma's geographical center, and astride the old Chisolm Trail.

2000 Population: 21,043

Notable Music History

BACK HOME WITH
GARTH BROOKS
IN CONCERT
SAT. FEB. 17, 1990 · 7:30 P.M.
YUKON HIGH SCHOOL AUDITORIUM

Along with over 100 years of polka music history relating to the Czech people who settled the area during the 1889 land run, the most significant musicians to come out of Yukon include now-"retired" country music superstar Garth Brooks and the red dirt group Cross Canadian Ragweed. For the better part of the1990s, Brooks was the biggest star of country music, and many say saved the industry when he became the biggest-selling single performer of all time, only re-eclipsed by Elvis Presley's sales in 2004.

Another group whose members were born elsewhere, but were raised primarily from Yukon, and who enjoyed nationwide success in 2004, is Cross Canadian Ragweed (pictured at right). A red dirt group who started as high school friends in Yukon, CCR regrouped in Stillwater while at Oklahoma State University, and now record for Universal-South Records.

Music Store

Visit CBR Music at 450 W. Main in Yukon and talk with owner Dale Klopfenstein, a guitarist born in Oklahoma City, who has opened for Johnny Cash and played with Oklahoma country music artists such as Henson Cargill.

Live Music Venues

Built in 1901, Czech Hall was constructed to preserve Czech lifeways, to include music and dance. Public dances are held every Saturday night 8:30 to midnight, with either the John Simpson Orchestra (right) or the Masopust Polka Band providing the music. Czech Hall is located at 205 N. Czech Hall Rd., Yukon, OK 73099 (2.5 miles south of Yukon on Cornwell Drive (aka Czech Hall Rd.). Smoke free environment. All ages welcome. $5.00 admission fee.Children under 13 admitted free. www.czechhall.com.

The 50 Yard Line Bar and Grill on Main Street, next door to CBR Music, occasionally features a live band or solo performer.

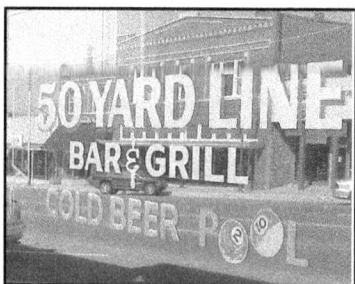

For Vinyl Collectors

Route 66 Traders Market has 57,000 square feet of space filled
with 200 booths. New and established vendors every week,
Open Sat. and Sunday, 9 am- 5 pm, www.rt66traders.com,
Route 66 and N. Richland Road, Yukon, (405) 350-3366.

Annual Musical Events in Yukon

Freedom Fest, July 4, live entertainment including a
performance by the Oklahoma City Philharmonic
City Parks, (405) 354-7208.
Annual Czech Festival, 1st Saturday in October, annual
celebration with Czech music and dancing, 5th and Cedar,
(405) 206-8142 or www.oklahomaczechfestival.com.

For More Information

Yukon Chamber of Commerce, 510 Elm, Yukon, 73099
(405) 354-3567 or www.yukoncc.com.

Cheyenne and Arapaho Tribes

Brief Tribal History

Two culturallay distinct
people, the Cheyenne and
Arapaho people have been
allied for centuries, at times

uneasily. The Arapaho name comes down from the Pawnee
term "tirapihu," or "he buys and trades," referring to the tribe's
trading status between northern and southern tribeson the Great
Plains. The Cheyenne name derives from the Sioux language,
"Shai-ena," or "people with a different speech." Like many
tribes, the Cheyenne's name for themselves indicates "our
people," or "people who are alike."

Starting the modern historical period on the Cheyenne

River region of North Dakota in the 1600s, the Cheyenne moved southward and were noted by Lewis and Clark in 1804 as being in the Black Hills of South Dakota. After a treaty with the U.S. government in 1825 that promised the tribe protection, half of the group moved to Colorado along the Arkansas River, becoming known as the Southern Cheyenne, while the Northern Cheyenne remained unsettled by government standards for another 50 years.

The Southern Cheyenne's "protection" by the U.S. Government did not go well, to say the least, and two events, the Massacre at Sand Creek in Colorado, and the Battle of the Washita in Oklahoma, both proved to be tragic events that illustrate the tension, racism, and lack of trust that existed between people on the Great Plains in the second half of the nineteenth century. Without providing an entire history of the Plains Indian Wars, which is done thoroughly elsewhere, the end result places the Southern Cheyenne on their reservation in western Oklahoma. After the allotment process in which tribal lands were divided up into acreages for tribal members, the remainder was opened for settlement in the now famous Oklahoma land runs.

The Arapaho's modern history first places them in permanent villages near the headwaters of the Mississippi River, and as far as the westernmost edge of Lake Superior, where they raised corn. The tribe eventually began migrating west, most likely in the 1600s with the introduction of the horse, when the Arapaho became buffalo hunters and tipi dwellers. The Arapaho's formal history with the Cheyenne dates to a joint treaty with the U.S. in 1861, and then follows a similar path through Colorado and Oklahoma to their current homes today in western Oklahoma.

Tribal Music Traditions

The Cheyenne and Arapaho both have a wealth of music traditions that include war dances and warrior society songs, Christian hymns, lullabies, peyote songs for the Native American Church, and the music that goes along with the Cheyenne Sun Dance, or Arapaho Sacred Pipe Ceremonies. As with many tribes in Oklahoma, rarely do outsiders have access to the traditional music of Cheyenne and Arapaho people, beyond what has been recorded for historic purposes. The most accessible musical activity is the annual Oklahoma Indian Nation Powwow, held the first weekend in August, that is free and open to the public.

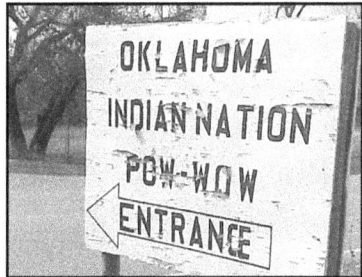

Annual Music Events

Oklahoma Indian Nation Powwow, 1st weekend of August, held behind the Cheyenne and Arapaho Tribal Headquarters. Drive west on the tree-lined road next to the Lucky Star Casino, circle around behind the tribal complex, and look for the powwow sign. Additionally, throughout the year various dances are scheduled throughout the Cheyenne & Arapaho Nation. Interested travelers should contact the tribal headquarters, or visit www.powwows.com for dance listings.

Tourist note of caution: At certain times of the year, travelers may notice a large wooden structure to the north of the service road leading to the tribal complex. This wooden structure is a sun dance arbor and is considered sacred to Cheyenne people. Under no circumstances should tourists park and approach the structure, nor should any photographs of the structure be taken. If C & A police see anyone near the structure taking pictures, officers are instructed to confiscate the film and/or video tape.

Live Music Venue

Lucky Star Casino, north of El Reno on Highway 81, is operated by the Cheyenne and Arapaho tribes to raise money for tribal programs. Occasionally, the casino features live music by local and national artists.

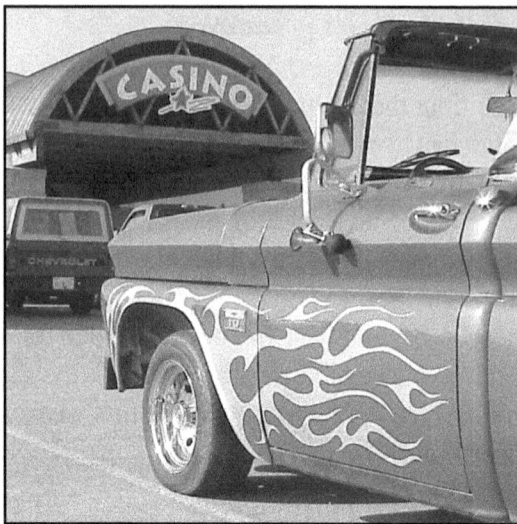

For More Information

Cheyenne & Arapaho Headquarters, (405) 262-0345.
Cheyenne Cultural Center, Clinton, 2250 NE SH 66
    (580) 323-6224.
Lucky Star Casino, www.luckystarcasino.org, (405) 262-7612.

El Reno

Established in 1874 as a cavalry outpost.

2000 Population: 16,212

Notable Music History

While the most notable and historic continuous music in the area is that of the Cheyenne and Arapaho tribes, the most significant musician from the area is avant-garde jazz saxophonist and composer Sam Rivers (pictured above), born in El Reno on September 25, 1930.

Sam Rivers was immersed in music at an early age as his father and mother, as well as grandparents were musicians, especially in the gospel genre. His father was a graduate of Fisk University and sang with the Fisk Jubilee Singers and the Silvertone Quartet, while his mother was a pianist who gave him lessons as early as four years old. Sam's grandfather wrote and published, in 1882, *A Collection of Revival Hymns and Plantation Melodies.* Before the family moved away from El Reno when he was twelve, Sam played soprano sax in the school band.

Music Stores

Clark's Hobby & Crafts
   211 S. Bickford
   El Reno, OK 73036
   (405) 262-1935

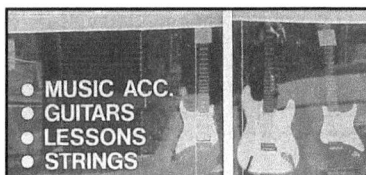

Visit Clark's Hobby and Crafts, which not only features guitars, but also beads, art supplies and model kits of all types.

Live Music Venue

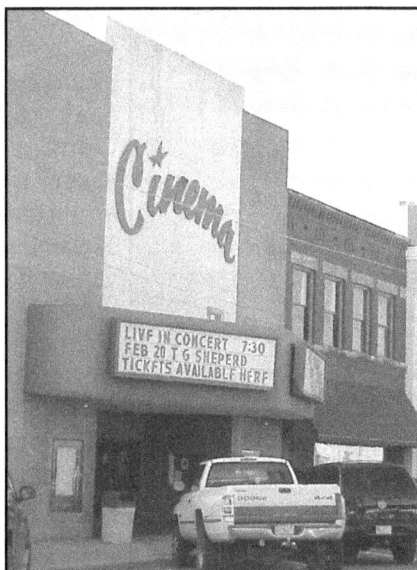

The El Reno Cinema has been converted into the Trolley Town Music Hall. Along with national touring acts, the hall , located at 110 S. Bickford, features regular Saturday evening performances of gospel, bluegrasss, and country music. For more information, call (405) 262-1900.

Historic Sites with a Musical Focus

Fort Reno, a military camp in 1874, was established as a military post in 1875. The Fort and Darlington Agency, which served Cheyenne and Arapaho people across the Canadian River, worked together to preserve peace on the Plains, as well direct the transition of this area from reservation land to individual farms and ranches. Troops from Fort Reno supervised the first land run of 1889 that opened the unassigned territory for settlement.

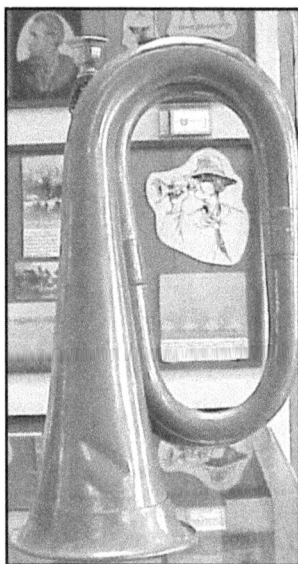

Along with a small museum that features the original cavalry bugle pictured at left, the fort also is the site of a chapel built by World War II German prisoners of war. Inside the chapel, which is open to the public, is an antique pump organ used in November on German Memorial Day. On this day, German songs are sung inside the chapel to memorialize the German POWS buried at Fort Reno. On the Sunday before Christmas, carols are sung in the chapel. Fort Reno is located west of El Reno, and travelers will locate signs easily along Route 66. For more information, call (405) 262-3987.

For Vinyl Collectors

Route 66 Antique Mall, 1629 E SH 66, is just west of El Reno and does have some 78 and 33 rpm vinyl. As with other flea markets and antique malls catering to tourists, however, discovering anything of note in a reasonable price range is unusual.

Annual Musical Events

'89ers Day, Last Saturday of April, living history re-enactors, period music, (405) 262-5121, www.elreno.org

Annual Burger Day Festival, first Saturday of May, downtown. This event revolves around the cooking a new world's largest onion-fried hamburger, weighing over 750 founds and reaching 8.5 feet in diameter. Live entertainment is featured. (405) 262-8888 or www.elreno.org.

Small Town Weekend, First weekend in June, Sunset Drive in El Reno. A classic car weekend with a live concert on Friday night, and a legal Route 66 "burnout" and closed cruise (vehicles 1982 and older). For more information, call (405) 262-3876, or see www.ercruisers.com.

El Reno Heritage and Arts Festival, September, downtown. Live entertainment. (405) 262-8888 or www.elreno.org

Tombstone Tales, September. See historic re-enactors portray individuals interred between 1874 and 1947 at the Fort Reno Post Cemetery. The stories of buffalo soldiers, Cheyenne scouts, German POWs, and settlers are told, and some period music is performed. For more information, call (405) 262-3987, or see www.fortreno.org.

For More Information

El Reno Chamber of Commerce, 206 N. Bickford, Box 67, 73036, (405) 262-1168, www.elrenochamber.com

El Reno Convention and Visitors Bureau, (888) 535-7366

Canadian County Historical Museum, 300 S. Grand, Wed-Sat. 10 a.m. to 5 p.m., Sun. 1 p.m. to 5 p.m. Free.

Calumet

Notable Music History

Aside from area churches, and members of the Cheyenne and Arapaho tribe who live in the area and are singers, the most significant musicians to come from Calumet include Roy Carter of the Chuck Wagon Gang gospel group, jazz guitarist Dempsey Wright (b. 1929), and Cross Canadian Ragweed bassist Jeremy Plato (pictured at right), who graduated from Calumet High School in 1994.

Live Music Venue

Aside from a few churches, the closest Calumet has to any live music is Davidson's Bar, which features karaoke on the weekends.

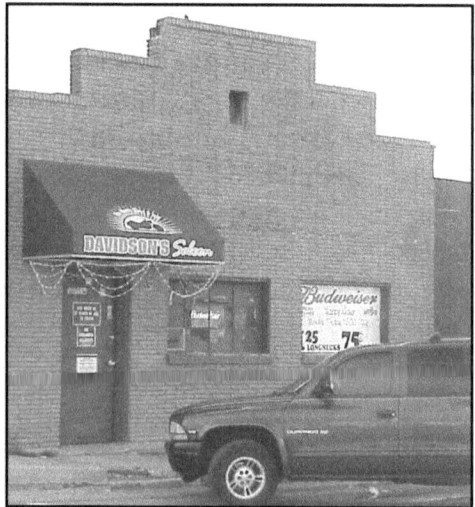

For More Information

Calumet Chamber of Commerce, (405) 893-2323.

Looking east about three miles from Geary on Historic Route 66, Coyote Hill is the site of the last Ghost Dance in this area of the Great Plains.

Historic Site with a Musical Focus

While neither Calumet nor Geary have been on Route 66 since 1933, they were part of the road's original alignment, and travelers can enjoy a nice drive from Calumet to Geary, or vice-versa. Of particular note on the north side of the road just east of Geary is Coyote Hill, one of the sites of the Ghost Dance revival of the 1890s. With this ceremony, Plains tribes hoped they could bring back the traditional way of life that was rapidly vanishing at the time. However, the Federal Government wanted no activities of this type happening on reservations. Subsequently, a cavalry detachment was sent from Fort Reno to break up the last Ghost Dance on Coyote Hill. The property is posted as belonging to the Oklahoma Department of Transportation. Contemporarily, the Cheyenne and Arapaho tribes do have Sun Dances at Concho and near Seiling each summer. in July.

Geary

Established: 1898   *2000 Population:* 1, 258

Live Music Venue

Like several other small towns along Hisoric Route 66 in Oklahoma, a local bar is the primary outlet for live music, or at least semi-live music. Jan's Place, on Main Street, features karaoke every weekend. Although Geary was not officially on the original route, the old postal route was, and enterprising townspeople put signs up indicating that Geary was just as much a part of the route as anyone else.

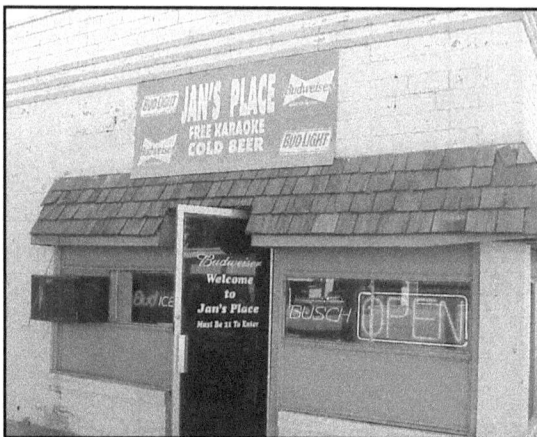

For More Information

Geary Chamber of Commerce, 120 E. Main, (405) 884-2765, or www.gearyok.com.

Canadian Rivers Historical Society Museum, 115 E. Main.

Technically, Geary is located within the Oklahoma Department of Tourism's definition of Red Carpet Country, or the northwest portion of the state that includes the Oklahoma panhandle. For more information on this area, see www.redcarpetcountry.com, or www.travelok.com, the state's official tourism site.

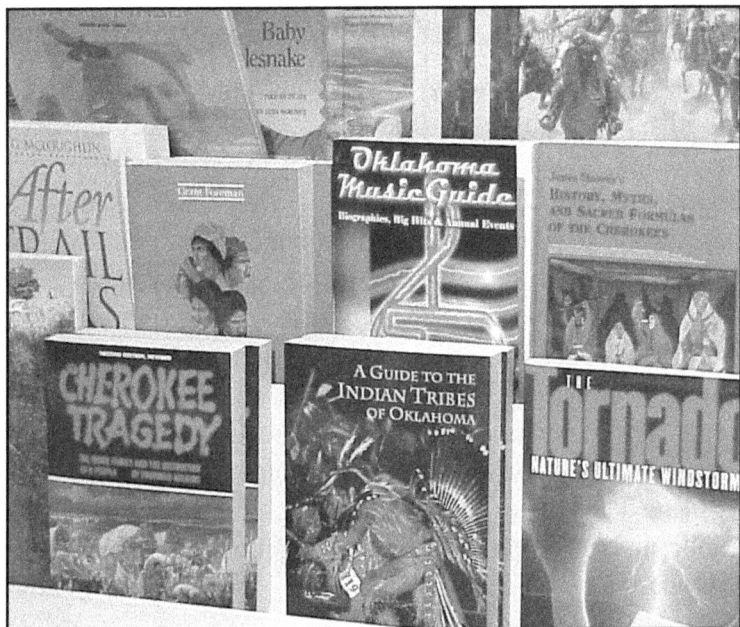

Should travelers decide not to take the dirt road alignment of old Route out of Geary to Bridgeport, they will be able to visit the much-advertised Cherokee Trading Post at the intersection of Highway 281 and Interstate 40. The trading post is a good place to collect authentic, handmade materials by local Native people, as well as books to flesh out the overall story of Oklahoma.

Wichita, Caddo, and Delaware Tribes

Between the west side of the Canadian River and the Custer County line just east of Weatherford, travelers are in the northernmost part of the Wichita, Caddo, and Delaware tribal jurisdiction, known locally as WCD.

Wichita and Affiliated Tribes

Brief Tribal History

With their own belief that they have been in the area forever, the Wichita are generally acknowledged to be one of the original tribes of Oklahoma, and, along with Caddo, are the descendants of people that built the mounds in eastern Oklahoma known as the Spiro Mounds. Spanish explorer Coronado made contact with the tribe in what is now southern Kansas in 1542, and noted that Wichita villages extended throughout much of Oklahoma to northeast and north-central Texas. Today, the tribe's headquarters are just north of Anadarko, about forty miles south of Route 66, where a small museum that doubles as a tribal meeting room is open to the public, and can be viewed if the meeting room is not being used. Call ahead for availability.

Tribal Music Traditions

The Wichita Tribe still has some of their traditional music intact, such as their friendship songs, ghost dance songs, dog dance songs, and big wolf songs, but rarely are they performed for non-Wichitas. For the most part, Wichita people are very much a part of the intertribal powwow traditions of southwestern Oklahoma. The tribe hosts many dances at their indoor dance hall and outdoor dance arbor at the tribal complex just north of Anadarko. Check the tribe's website for dance announcements.

Annual Music Events

Annual Wichita Tribal Dance, Second Weekend of August, Wichita Tribal Complex.

For More Information

Wichita and Affiliated Tribes, Box 729, Anadarko, 73005, (405) 247-2430, www.wichita.nsn.us.

Caddo Nation
Brief Tribal History

The Caddo tribe's history over the last thousand years has been well documented; however, significant archaeological evidence places the people in the southeastern Oklahoma region nearly 10,000 years ago. First, the Caddo, along with the Wichita, are commonly associated with the moundbuilders who constructed what are known as the Spiro Mounds in eastern Oklahoma. However, after the demise of that particular mound complex, the Caddo moved south into the four corners area of Oklahoma, Texas, Arkansas, and Louisiana, while the Wichita moved west, and then spread out north and south to cover the a wide swath of present-day Kansas, Oklahoma, and Texas.

The Caddo Nation traded with the French and Spanish who claimed the Louisiana Territory until it was purchased by the U.S. in 1803. In the resulting expansion of the U.S., and creation of Texas, the Caddo were forced out of their tribal homelands. After a series of moves and the Civil War, they located permanently on the Wichita Reservation in Indian Territory in 1867; and, in 1874, the U.S. Government delineated the northern half of the reservation (through which Route 66 currently runs) as the Caddo Reservation. In 1902, tribal members received 160 acre allotments, and the rest was

Tribal Music Traditions

Caddo people are involved in practically every element of traditional, pan-Indian (powwow), and Christian American Indian music. Traditionally, Caddo people maintain their traditional Turkey Dance and, additionally, some Caddo people are members of the Native American Church and have specific Caddo songs to relate to that form of worship. Caddos have also long been involved in the intertribal, pan-Indian powwow world, with some of the first intertribal dances outside of fairs and Wild West shows taking place on Caddo family land as early as 1918.

Historic Sites with a Musical Focus
Caddo Nation Heritage Museum, open Monday through
  Friday from 9 a.m. to 4:30 p.m.

Annual Music Events
Annual Turkey Dance

Caddo Drum Group, 2000

For More Information
Caddo Nation Headquarters, Box 487, Binger, 73009,
  (405) 656-2344 or www.caddonation-nsn.us.

Western Delaware
Brief Tribal History
  With their land base at the time of European contact an area that included present-day New Jersey, Pennsylvannia, New York, and Delaware, the Delaware signed the first treaty with the United States in 1778. Over the course of the next forty years, as their lands became the states previously mentioned, the tribe eventually made their way through a series of moves to Indian Territory (Oklahoma) in 1812. By 1820, two bands made their way to Texas where they allied with the Wichita and Caddo tribes. All three were moved north in 1859 to an area designated for the three tribes along the Washita River that comprised the reservation before it was split between the Caddo and Wichita.

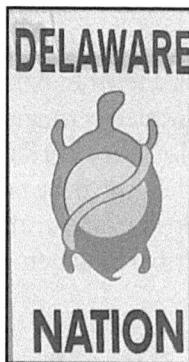

Tribal Music Traditions

Most Western Delaware people are either involved in the intertribal powwow world, or sing in Christian churches.

For More Information

Western Delaware Tribal Headquarters, Box 825, Anadarko, 73005, (405) 247-9393.
Western Delaware Tribal Museum, located at the tribal headquarters about four miles north of Anadarko.

.

Bridgeport

Established formally in 1898 when the Rock Island Railroad built a bridge to cross the Canadian River.
2000 Population: 109

Laura Lee McBride   "Queen of Western Swing"

Born: May 20, 1920 ,in Bridgeport
Died: January 25, 1989
Notability: Born on a farm near Bridgeport, and known as the "Queen of Western Swing" because she was the first female vocalist with a Western swing group, Bob Wills and the Texas Playboys, Laura Frances Owens was the daughter of Maude and D. H. "Tex" Owens, composer of the country music classic "Cattle Call." Her father gave up his occupation as a mechanic to devote his career to music, and the family moved to Kansas City, Missouri, where "Tex" launched his own radio show on KMBC. Laura Lee's first public performance was at age ten with her sister, teaming as "Joy and Jane" on their father's radio program.

For More Information

Bridgeport City Hall, (405) 542-6004.

Musical Side Trips

Bridgeport is the logical point to turn south and visit Anadarko's Indian City, as well as other points of interest in

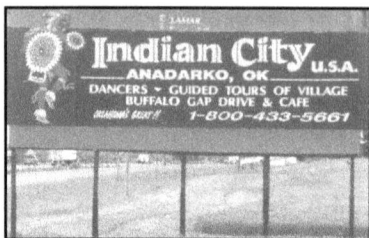

Anadarko, such as the Southern Plains Indian Museum, and the American Indian Hall of Fame. In addition to the museums operated by the Caddo in Binger and the Wichita and Western Delaware north of Anadarko, the Apache Tribe of Oklahoma is also located in Anadarko. The Apache have a nice selection of hand made items in their convenience store and gift shop just south of Anadarko on Highway 8 before the turnoff to Indian City.

Hydro

Established: 1898   **2000 Population:** 1,060

Notable Area Musicians

Along with Blaine Greteman of the country-rock group Delicious Militia, who was born in Oklahoma City, but was graduated from high school in Hydro, country singer/songwriter Bo Lightfoot currently bases his entertainment operation in Hydro.

Live Music Venues

Along with the Graffit Grill at 206 W. Main that features occasional coffee house type singers and groups, the Hydro Bar has karaoke or a live band every Saturday night.

For More Information

Hydro Chamber of Commerce, (405) 663-2531.

Musical Side Trips

Kiowa Gourd Clan, Carnegie, July 3rd and 4th. For travelers interested in an authentic Plains tribe ceremony, the Kiowa Gourd Clan Ceremonies take place July 3rd and 4th every year in Carnegie Park. The public is welcome to view these activities, with the only caution being the weather is usually hot, and there is very little shade for non-campers. Attending in the evening guarantees some cooler temperatures. As with most outdoor American Indian activities, travelers are advised to bring a lawn chair, and to not take photographs or videos without asking first at the speaker's stand. For the uninitiated, this dance and ceremony is related to ancient Kiowa ways that date to the time of the Sun Dance before the Federal Government outlawed all Plains ceremonies of this nature in the late nineteenth century. Now, the gourd dance has grown beyond the Kiowa to become an intertribal dance at powwows across the U.S. and Canada. While the Kiowa do not necessarily approve of these activities, elders are resigned to the fact it is going on, and only hope people will be respectful of the dance, its songs, and its protocol.

For tourists who can not make the Gourd Clan activities, the Kiowa museum located at the tribal headquarters in Carnegie is a good introduction to Kiowa lifeways and history.

For More Information

Kiowa Tribe, (580) 654-2300, Box 369, Carnegie, 73015.

Weatherford

Established March 6, 1898, as the Rock Island Railroad continued building stops westward in the former Cheyenne and Arapaho lands, having made it across the Canadian at Bridgeport.

2000 Population: 9,859

Notable Music History

Along with being the birthplace of legendary Bob Wills guitarist, Eldon Shamblin, Weatherford is also home to Gordon Friesen. Friesen married noted folksinger Agnes "Sis" Cunningham, herself from nearby Watonga, thirty-seven miles via highway northwest of Weatherford, where her future husband lived and where she would attend college.

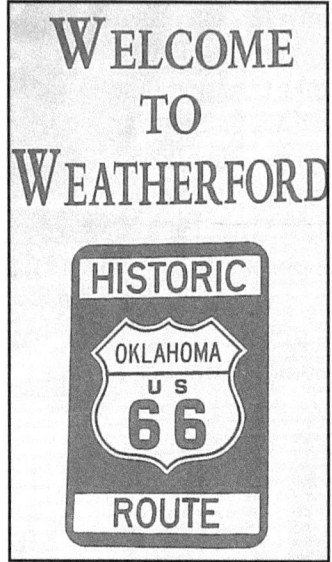

WELCOME TO WEATHERFORD

HISTORIC OKLAHOMA US 66 ROUTE

A founding member of Oklahoma's Red Dust Players, singer and accordionist with the Almanac Singers, and co-founder and editor of *Broadside: The Topical Folk Song Magazine*, Agnes "Sis" Cunningham was born on a farm near Watonga. Agnes' parents had homesteaded on the former Cheyenne-Arapaho Indian Reservation and began farming on the banks of the North Canadian River; however, the soil was sandy, and they moved to another farm with better land closer to Watonga. The middle of five children (two older brothers and a younger brother and sister), Agnes helped her mother raise chickens, tend the vegetable garden, and clean house. When Agnes was six, her father, William "Chick" Cunningham, taught her to play chords on the piano, and she would stop at her grandmother's house after school in Watonga to practice. Her father was an old-time fiddler and claimed to know more than 500 fiddle tunes. Politically, he was a Debs Socialist. One of her brothers, William, a 1925 journalism graduate of the University of Oklahoma, became state director of the Oklahoma's Writers Project in 1935.

While in high school, Agnes joined the debate team and started a school newspaper, *The Shotgun*, which gave her journalistic experience that served her well later as an editor. She was a voracious reader in high school, including such authors as Dickens (*Tale of Two* Cities), Dreiser (*Sister Carrie*), and Sinclair (*The Jungle*). Her mother had taught school for eight years, so when Agnes graduated from high school, she enrolled at Weatherford Teachers' College (later Southwestern Oklahoma State University) in 1927 to become a teacher. She completed two years, and began teaching music at age twenty.

In the summer of 1931 Agnes attended the Commonwealth College near Mena, Arkansas, an unaccredited labor college with socialist tendencies. Her brother Bill was director of the college and his wife was on the faculty. It was here that Agnes began writing songs, such as "Sundown" and "There Are Strange Things Happening in This Land," which her father helped compose. Following Commonwealth, Agnes became an organizer for the Southern Tenant Farmers' Union and served as a delegate to its convention in Muskogee, Oklahoma, in 1937. She then left Oklahoma for the next two years, and taught music and directed the singing of labor songs at the Southern Labor School for Women near Asheville, North Carolina.

In 1939 Cunningham returned to her native state to help organize the Red Dust Players, a musical and acting troupe formed to present topical skits and songs for sharecroppers and union workers around Oklahoma. During her two years with the Red Dust Players she continued to write songs, such as "The Oil Derrick Out by West Tulsa," reflecting the oil workers strike at the Mid-Continent Refinery of the DX Oil Company near

Tulsa. It was during her two-year tenure with the Red Dust Players that she met Woody Guthrie and Pete Seeger when they came through Oklahoma City to visit Woody's wife and children. While at a union meeting in Oklahoma City, Woody wrote "Union Maid."

Sis met Gordon Friesen, a Weatherford boy, in March of 1941, through their association with the Communist Party, and they married on July 23. Fearing repercussions from their Communist activities, Sis and Gordon moved to New York City the following November. Once there, Pete Seeger invited them to move into the Almanac House at 130 West 10th Street. A year earlier, Seeger, Lee Hays, and Millard Lampell had formed the Almanac Singers, the first urban folk singing group in America, and they invited Sis to join. The Almanac Singers consisted of several musicians, including at various times, Woody Guthrie, Bess Lomax, Peter Hawes, Cisco Houston, Arthur Stern, Josh White, and Burl Ives. Sis appeared on the Almanac Singers 1942 album *Dear Mr. President,* released by Keynote Records. Her contribution was "Belt Line Girls," a song she had written urging women to help in the war effort. Several of the Almanac Singers either enlisted or were drafted into the military services as the U.S. entered World War II.

In late 1942, Sis and Gordon moved to Detroit to assist Bess Lomax and others to organize another branch of the Almanac Singers, but the attempt failed, and Sis went to work in a war plant and Gordon became a reporter for the *Detroit Times*. In 1944 they returned to New York, where daughters Agnes and Jane were born in 1945 and 1949, respectively. By this time Gordon was blacklisted and could find no steady employment. He and Sis took turns taking care of the girls and working part time jobs. During this tough period, Sis wrote two of her most remembered songs, "Mister Congressman" and "Fayette County."

In 1961 Pete Seeger returned from a tour of England where he had witnessed a renewed interest in writing songs dealing with the political and social issues of the day. He visited with West Coast folksinger Malvina Reynolds about starting a publication that would print new folks songs concerned with current topics. When Reynolds decided to concentrate on her own singing and writing career, Seeger turned to Sis and Gordon; and in 1962 the first mimeographed issue of *Broadside* was printed. The first edition contained six songs, including "Talking John Birch Society" by a yet unknown Bob Dylan. It was the first Dylan song to appear in print. *Broadside* continued to showcase the work of Dylan. "Blowin' in the Wind," for example, appeared in the magazine nearly a year before Peter, Paul, and Mary recorded it. Other young folk songwriters followed, including Phil Ochs, Janis Ian, Tom Paxton, Buffy Ste. Marie, and Peter LaFarge. *Broadside* published not only the songs of the new generation of songwriters, but also those of the older writers, such as Pete Seeger and Malvina Reynolds. With financial assistance from Pete and Toshi Seeger, *Broadside* continued until 1988, sometimes publishing irregularly, either monthly, bimonthly, or quarterly, but for twenty-six years it provided an opportunity for folk music enthusiasts to learn the songs of both new and old songwriters. Throughout those years, it was Sis who transcribed the music in order to print the music notations into the magazine. It was Sis who took part in hootenannies to help support the magazine. Finally, she recorded a full album of her songs, *Sundown,* released by Folkways Records in 1976 as *Broadside Ballads, Volume 9* that has been re-mastered by Smithsonian Folkways Recordings as *Agnes "Sis" Cunningham Sings Her Own Songs and A Few Old Favorites. The Original Talking Union with the Almanac Singers* was released by Folkways Records in 1955 and has been digitally re-mastered in CD format by Smithsonian Folkways Records.

Sis contributed three tracks ("Sundown," "My Oklahoma Home (It Blowed Away)," and "But If I Ask Them") to the *Best of Broadside, 1962-1988* album released in 2000. In

1999, Ronald Cohen, historian and folk music scholar, edited *Red Dust and Broadsides: A Joint Autobiography* of Agnes "Sis" Cunningham and Gordon Friesen. Gordon died in 1996; but Agnes, now in her 90s, lives in a senior citizens home in Modina, New York. Daughter Jane lives in New Paltz, New York, near Agnes, and daughter Agnes lives in Berkeley, California.

SWOSU Music Dept.

As a result of Southwestern Oklahoma State University being located in Weatherford, primary non-church musical activities in town focus on the school's music program, and the students who form bands while they are in school. Several such bands exist, to include Solomon's Splendor (Christian rock), Sub Seven (hardcore), Walrus (rock jamband), Banner Road (Christian rock)., and Jackson after the Accident (pop/rock).

In other genres, fiddler Joe Helser and country singer/guitarist T.J. Caulkins are based in town, as is Derek McCarver, who sings and plays guitar at the Oklahoma Opry in OKC. Powwow headsingers the Watan Brothers live in Weatherford, and of particular recent distinction is Charles Chapman, who retired in 2004 after forty-two years teaching in SWOSU's music department. However, perhaps no one from Weatherford has had more impact than Eldon Shamblin.

In 1937, Eldon Shamblin joined Bob Wills and his Texas Playboys. Once with Wills, Shamblin began providing a completely unique sound on guitar by duplicating bass lines on the bass strings of the guitar while playing chords of tunes on the tenor strings. Shamblin maneuvered the the guitar into a frontline solo position in the group and was the Western swing representation of the guitar sound evolving in Oklahoma City via jazz giant Charlie Christian. One of Wills' best biographers,

Charles R. Townsend, in his excellent account of Wills' career *San Antonio Rose: The Life and Music of Bob Wills*, speculates Christian heard Shamblin's work over KVOO in 1938 and began emulating some of Shamblin's work. Whatever similarities and cross-fertilization occurred between Shamblin and Christian, the two musicians who matured in Oklahoma were intrinsic to the developing the significance of the electric guitar as a

Eldon Shamblin

frontline instrument in American popular music. Shamblin's significant duet recordings with steel guitarist Leon McAuliffe on "Bob Wills Special" and "Twin Guitar Special" are Western swing standards and benchmarks of the country music substyle. By the twentieth century's end, *Rolling Stone* magazine called Eldon the world's greatest rhythm guitarist, and *Musician* magazine declared him one of the twenty prime movers in guitar history.

Music Store

Midwest Music,
811 E. Main,
Weatherford, 73096,
(580) 772-2237.

Not only does Midwest Music have the best marching band equipment selection on Route 66 in Oklahoma, the store has an interesting collection of guitars, and a freaky-looking dummy dressed up in a band uniform. Most of the young people who work in the store play in a local band. To find out what's going on in the Weatherford scene or buy an independent CD from a local group, stop in here.

Guitar racks at Midwest Music in Weatherford

Live Music Venues in Weatherford

One Eighty, a converted movie theatre at 200 W. Main, does show movies occasionally, but is primarily a Christian pop and rock outlet. Call (580) 772-7825 for scheduling.

J.C. Cowboys, west of town at Exit 80 on the north side of I-40, is a country music dance club, with live bands often on the weekends. At right, SWOSU is pictured on the hill in the background, looking north across I-40. Call (580) 772-2851 for info.

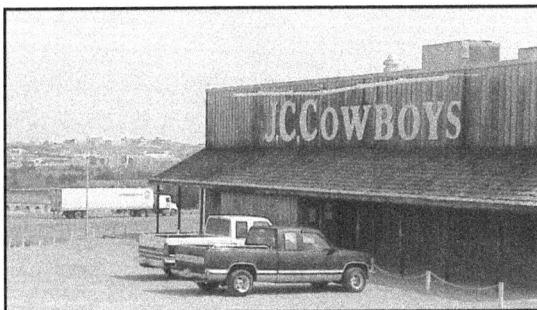

Annual Musical Events

Annual SWOSU Jazz Festival, since 1970, February, (580) 774-3708 or www.swosu.edu

Southwestern Festival of the Arts, live music, September, Means Park, Weatherford, (580) 772-1610.

For More Information

Weatherford Area Chamber of Commerce, Room 224, City Hall, Box 857, Weatherford, 73096, (800) 725-7744, or www.weatherfordchamber.com.

Weatherford Daily News, www.wdnonline.com

One thing about driving out west, one missed turn can put travlers on a whole new adventure, such as this road west of Weatherford that finished off in a dead end near Clinton. However, after we doubled back and found a main road to I-40, we "discovered" the Country Jamboree just east of Clinton,

and north of the Cherokee Trading Post on I-40. Featuring country and western music on the first and third Saturday nights of each month, and gospel music every fifth Saturday, Country Jamboree is no secret to bus tours of people who ride in from Oklahoma City and elsewhere to enjoy the high quality music and pleasant atmosphere. Call (405) 929-7273 for more information.

Clinton

Established: 1903 as the next Rock Island Railroad stop.
2000 Population: 8,833

Notable Music History

Along with the Oklahoma Route 66 Museum, and being the site of a hotel room where Elvis Presley slept several times in the late 1960s and 1970s, Clinton has made some very prominent contributions to country and western music. A half century ago, guitarists Junior Keith (Bob Wills circa 1950s) and Tommy Elliot (Johnnie Lee Wills circa 1950s), as well as Bob Wills' 1950s era manager Lucky Moeller, were all from Clinton. More recently, the town is the birthplace of country music producer Scott Hendricks and modern roughneck country superstar Toby Keith.

Having produced over thirty songs that have gone to #1 on *Billboard*'s Hot Country Singles chart, Scott Hendricks is one of Nashville's most important music producers. Football fans probably don't know that Hendricks engineered and produced the original Monday Night Football theme recorded by Hank Williams, Jr., for which Hendricks won an Emmy in 1992. A graduate of Oklahoma State in Stillwater, Scott moved to Nashville in the late 1970s where his first successful venture was with Restless Heart, a group for whom Hendricks produced six #1 hits.

Hendricks has also produced for Alan Jackson, Brooks and Dunn, Faith Hill, Trace Adkins, Asleep at the Wheel, and Aaron Tippin, as well as producing one installment of the Roy D. Mercer *How Big a Boy Are You* series of comedy CDs by the Tulsa morning show duo of Phil and Brent. (Occasionally, by the way, travelers can hear original, new Roy D. Mercer recordings, and old favorites, on 97.5 FM, KMOD in Tulsa, weekdays 6 a.m to 10 a.m.).

Toby Keith   Country singer/songwriter
Born: July 8, 1961, in Clinton where his father worked for the highway department.

Musical Notability: As one of contemporary country music's superstars, Toby Keith (left) could fill up several pages here with self-composed #1 hits ("I Should've Been a Cowboy," "Who's Your Daddy?" "Beer for My Horses" with Willie Nelson, and "I Love this Bar" - 16 total), not to mention a #1 for most concert tickets sold in 2002, a fact which also helped him earn *Billboard*'s Country Artist of the Year in 2002. Sales of his tenth album *Shock 'N Y'All* (Dreamworks, 2003) keep adding to his already impressive sales total of more than 13.5 million. Even with the large sales, major awards shows, like the ones given by the Country Music Association (CMA), have looked away from Keith's rough-hewn individualism. Keith does not fit the polished model of modern Nashville pop.

   In essence, he is thought of as an Okie in the worst way by the Nashville establishment. However, given his background in western, rural Oklahoma, one shouldn't be surprised to see Keith as one of another in a long line of country music artists who have been able to parlay their ordinary roots in the state to a nationwide connection with people for whom the glitz and glam of contemporary media and multi-national corporations do not reflect the average lifestyle of working class people, not to mention the typically conservative, or at least overtly patriotic, political leanings of the demographic that has always been the bedrock of country music's fan base. On his own terms, Toby Keith now writes and sings for that audience.

Music Store

As with most other independent music stores in smaller cities, Southwest Music owner Rob Howell also has a counter full of independent music releases by Clinton musicians, such as Hispanic Christian artist Ric Rodriguez and country singer Steven Penner. Additionally, if travelers want to get real insight into music history of the whole southwest, talk with pianist John Fortner, who is also a part-time teacher, and instrument technician at the store.

Born in Putnam, twenty-four miles north of Clinton and raised near Arapaho, just four miles north of Clinton, John Fortner played piano with Roy Clark, Norma Jean of Wellston, and gospel greats the Stamps Quartet. While enjoying his ranch north of town, he takes time for one gig per week at the First Methodist Church, 1001 Frisco Avenue, on Tuesdays for lunch. Southwest Music is located at

1424 Gary Boulevard, Clinton, 73601, or call (405) 323-4005.

Live Music Venues

Clinton American Legion Hut, 1971 South 4th, Clinton, country music dance every Friday, 7:30 p.m. to 10:30 p.m., (405) 323-5504.

Southwest Playhouse Fine Arts Center, 6th and Nowahy, Clinton, (405) 323-4448.

Arnold's, at 4th and Frisco, books live bands on weekends.

Administered by the Oklahoma Historical Society, The Route 66 Museum in Clinton offers a guided tour through a wonderful collection of Route 66 memorabilia and memories. Noted Route 66 author Michael Wallis narrates the journey through the decade-themed rooms of the museum that depict the road from its dirt road status to its current mythological status. Music of the various periods is featured throughout the museum. The Oklahoma Route 66 Museum is located off I-40 at Exit 65, 2229 Gary Boulevard, Clinton, 73601. Call (580) 323-RT66 for more information.

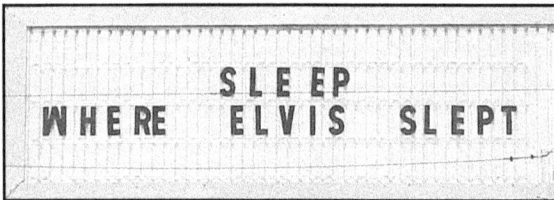

Hard to believe? Maybe, but it's true. Elvis Presley liked this low-key Best Western as a midway point between Memphis and Las Vegas or California. Elvis's advance people liked the hotel because Clinton was a quiet spot just off the interstate. Right across the street from the Route 66 Museum, the hotel room is decorated with a 1970s interior "as it was" when Elvis slept in the room. Booking the room (at right) is difficult, however, as travelers from around the world enjoy staying here. Call Best Western Tradewinds, (800) 528-1234.

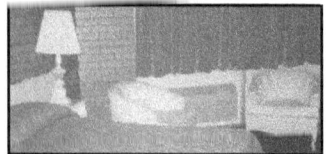

This is to certify that

Hugh Foley

of _Stillwater, Oklahoma_

Slept where Elvis slept

In the Elvis Suite of

BEST WESTERN TRADEWINDS INN
Clinton, Oklahoma

This is the motel accommodation used by Elvis Presley on several occasions as his entourage crossed the country filling engagements.

March 16 2004
Date

Signature of Innkeeper

Previous page: The certificate travelers are issued when staying in the "Elvis Room" (right) at the Clinton Best Western Tradewinds Inn.

Travelers are welcome at the Cheyenne Cultural Center at 2250 NE State Highway 66 on the east side of Clinton. The center features cultural exhibits by Cheyenne artisans, traveling exhibits, and seaonal activities, to include powwows and honor dances in the covered dance pavilion at the center. Open most weekdays from 9 a.m. to 5 p.m. Call (580) 323-6224.

For More Information About Clinton

Clinton Chamber of Commerce, 101 S. 4th, 73601, (580) 323-4572, or www.clintonok.org.

Foss

Established: 1902
2000 Population: 127
Live Music Venue

With a town this small, it's no surprise the main music in town is at the Foss Baptist Church, built in 1895, Sunday mornings at 11 a.m. For more information call Foss City Hall at (580) 592-4513, but only on Wednesday.

Canute

Established in 1901 as a Rock Island railroad station, and named after the ancient King of Denmark.

2000 Population: 524

Notable Music History

If anything, Canute is another unfortunate example of what happens to a town when the life force of its arteries dries up. Aside from its churches, Canute's only tangible evidence of music history is the former Tip Top Nightclub, pictured above as the far right building in this complex.

For More Information

Canute City Hall, 6th and Highway 66, (580) 472-3111

Elk City

Established: 1901

2000 Population: 10,510

The National Route 66 Museum is in Clinton, featuring a "walk through" of all eight states on the Mother Road.

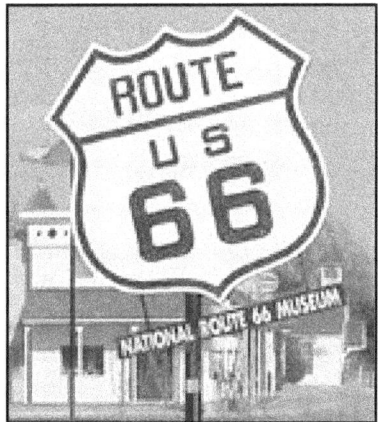

Notable Music History

While Jimmy Webb (right), author of "By the Time I Get to Phoenix," "McArthur Park, "Galveston," and "Wichita Lineman," is Elk City's best-known home-grown musician, several other names can be chiseled into the city's contributory slate of musical talent.

First, John Herren, keyboardist with the 1960s psychedelic outfit, The Electric Prunes, is an Elk City native. Then, Trader Price, a modern country group from the area, has enjoyed some national success as a result of the Price Brothers' longtime dedication to that group. Brothers Chris (keyboards, guitar), Dan (bass), and Erick (drums) are all from nearby Burns Flat and have played together for several years, at one time opening for Reba McEntire on her tours of the early 1990s. Chris Price also earned a GRAMMY for co-writing a song with Roy Orbison, "Lovin' You Feelin' Again." Another local country group, Slidebar, consists of primary members Buddy and Lyle Parman.

ELK CITY, OKLAHOMA'S 17TH ANNUAL

BLUEGRASS JAM

FREE   FREE

Friday & Saturday · March 19th & 20th, 2004

A/l Night Jammin!

Holiday Inn
Exit 38, I-40, Elk City, Oklahoma

ACOUSTIC INSTRUMENTS ONLY

Larry Nance
580-225-4139

Larry Ford
580-488-3822
(Business)
580-488-2984
(Residence)

Annual Musical Events

Annual Bluegrass Jam, March, (580) 225-4139.

Far West Fiddlers Convention, April, (580) 225-4363.

Music Stores

Wilson Musi c and Sound
  915 E. 3rd (Route 66)
  Elk City, OK 73644
  (580) 225-1996

Wilson Music and Sound
is just a block east of the
big, canted Route 66 sign
in front of the Old Town
Museum complex.
Owner Charles Eddy
(right) is an accomplished
guitarist and songwriter
on his own, having
toured with Trader Price in the late 1980s and early 1990s, as
well as leading his own group, Coyote Blue in the 1980s. The
store is well stocked with strings, music books, and plenty of
young players hanging around so visitors can find out what else
might be going on around town musically.

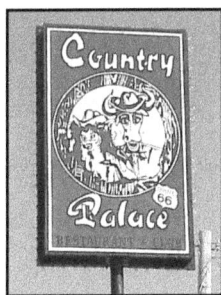

Live Music Venue

The primary live music venue in Elk City is
Country Palace at 2707 E. Highway 66,
east of town at Exit 41. For details about
bands playing on the weekends, call (580)
243-6538.

For Vinyl Collectors

Several antique stores in Elk City periodically carry vinyl. Try
Old Route 66 Antique Mall at 401 E. 3rd.

For More Information

Elk City Chamber 1016 Airport Blvd., 73648
  (800) 280-0207, www.elkcitychamber.com

Sayre

Established in 1902 as yet another westward stop on the Rock Island Railroad, the depot now serves as the current Short Grass Country Museum and Sayre Historical Society Office.

2000 Population: 4,114

Best Jukebox in Town
Route 66 Bar

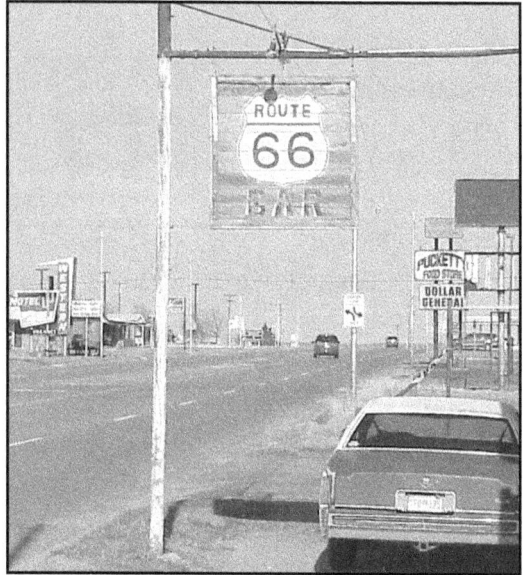

Annual Musical Events
The Route 66 Hoot and Scoot is the first weekend in October and features live entertainment, all-wheels car show, vendors, and food in the downtown square on Route 66.

Call (580) 928-2514 for details.

For More Information

Sayre Chamber of Commerce, 117 N. 4th, (580) 928-3386, www.sayreok.net.

Short Grass Country Museum, 106 E. Poplar, Rock Island Depot, free, open by appointment at (580) 928-5757, or (580) 928-5735.

Erick

Established in 1901 and named after Beeks Erick, the president of a townsite management company preparing the location for the oncoming Rock Island Railroad.

2000 Population: 1,023

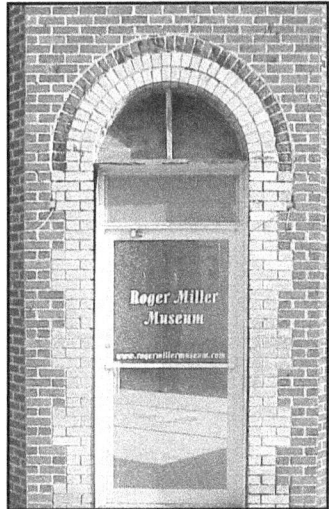

Notable Music History

Even the most casual Route 66 traveler tends to know that both Sheb Wooley and Roger Miller are from Erick, with Wooley being born in 1921 on a farm near town, and Miller arriving at age one in 1937. Best known musically for "The Purple People Eater," which has sold more than 100 million copies worldwide, Sheb Wooley was also a TV star for eight years in *Rawhide* (1959-1967) and appeared on many other shows, such as *Lassie*, *Cheyenne*, and *The Lone Ranger.* Roger Miller, of course, is known for several 1960s hits, such as "King of the Road," "Dang Me," "England Swings," and "Little Green Apples."

Given Roger Miller's popularity, the Erick Chamber of Commerce established a fund to begin the contruction of a Roger Miller Museum to house memorabilia, and materials relating to his life and career. The Chamber obtained a building at the corner of Roger Miller Boulevard and Sheb Wooley Street and expected to have it open by summer, 2004.

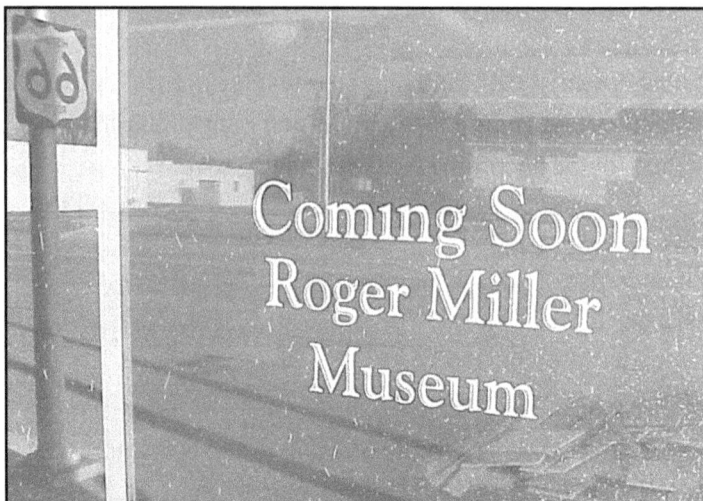

The Roger Miller Museum, under construction in March, 2004, opened in August, 2004. Museum hours are Wed. through Sat. from 1p.m to 5p.m. or call (580) 526-3833 for an appointment Write Box 1232, Erick, 73645 or see www.rogermiller.com

Miller, Roger Dean   Country/Pop Singer, Songwriter

Born: January 2, 1936 in Dallas, moved to Erick at age one

Died: October 25, 1992 in Nashville

The witty Roger Miller will always be known for his ability to bring light-hearted sensibility to heavy life subjects. His skills as a songwriter and singer culminated in the 1960s, with major pop and country hits such as "Dang Me," "England Swings," "King of the Road," "Little Green Apples," and "Chug-a-Lug." Born in Fort Worth, Texas, Roger's father Jean Miller died at twenty-six when Roger was only a year old. As a result, Roger's mother, Laudene Holt Miller, sent her three boys to live with Jean's brothers, and Roger wound up with Armelia and Elmer Miller on a farm outside the tiny southwestern Oklahoma town of Erick.

Although fifteen years older than Roger, Erick native Sheb Wooley, who later had a hit with "The Purple People Eater," taught Roger his first chords on guitar, bought him his first fiddle, and spent a lot of time listening to the radio that brought them the Grand Ole Opry on Saturday nights and the Light Crust Doughboys from Fort Worth by day. The connection also provided Sheb the opportunity to meet his wife Melva Miller Roger's cousin, which probably explains some of the closeness between the two. Filled with the hopes of youth and desperate to escape Erick at the end of the Depression-ravaged 1930s, Roger traveled Oklahoma and Texas, working where he could, and learning what he could in the honky tonks at night. He could not make enough money to buy a needed guitar, so he stole one in Texas and brought it back into Oklahoma. His conscience got the best of him though and he turned himself in to a judge who offered Miller an opportunity to enlist in the U.S. Army. After some hard lessons in Korea in 1952, Miller returned to the states and played fiddle in a Special Services group called the Circle A Wranglers at Fort McPherson, Georgia. After getting his discharge in 1956, Roger took off for Nashville where he had an unsuccessful audition with Chet Atkins and began washing dishes at the Andrew Jackson Hotel, smack in the middle of Nashville's country music scene.

Roger's first break came as fiddler in Minnie Pearl's road band, and his second professional opportunity occurred when he met George Jones at WSM radio one night. Roger played George some songs, and Jones then introduced Miller to Don Pierce and Pappy Daily of Mercury-Starday Records. The meeting led to a record deal in which Miller recorded his first single, "My Pillow" backed with "Poor Little John." Although the single had no success, Roger rode to the Texas session with George Jones and the two co-wrote some songs along the way, to include "Tall, Tall Trees," which Jones recorded in 1957, and "Happy Child," which Jimmy Dean also recorded the same year. The lack of significant success urged Miller to move out to Amarillo, Texas only a couple of hours west from Erick, and his wife pregnant with his first child. He joined the Amarillo Fire Department where he worked during the day, and played

Amarillo nightspots to further his dreams. Miller certainly drew from the period for the opening lines of "Dang Me," but the relocation also proved fortuitous when Miller met Ray Price one night at a club in Amarillo. Several months later, Price hired Roger to replace singer Van Howard in the Cherokee Cowboys, and the family was on their way back to Nashville. In the meantime, Miller had written "Invitation to the Blues," and the song made its way to singing cowboy Rex Allen, who had a hit with it in 1958. As Allen's version started to succeed, Miller suggested Ray Price cover the song and it became a #3 country hit. Roger also entered his first songwriting deal in 1958 with Tree Publishing and Buddy Killen, a Grand Ole Opry bassist Roger met in a Nashville bar. The two began a life-long friendship that saw Roger Miller rise to the heights of the country and pop music worlds.

With Killen getting his songs to artists, Roger began a string of country hits as a songwriter. Ernest Tubb hit with "Half a Mind" (#8); Faron Young

made the Top Ten with "That's the Way I Feel"; Jim Reeves took Miller's "Billy Bayou" to #1 and followed it a few months later with "Home" (#2). Even though Miller was having hits vicariously through other artists, he still wanted his own deal and landed one in 1958 on Decca Records, for which he recorded an unsuccessful honky tonk single "A Man Like Me," with Donny Little, later known as Johnny Paycheck, on harmony vocals. After leaving Ray Price's group, Roger joined Faron Young as drummer, and soon thereafter signed with RCA-

Nashville, run by the legendary guitarist and architect of the Nashville pop sound, or, depending on one's perspective, the man who genericized country music, Chet Atkins.

In 1960, Miller's first single of that year was "You Don't Want My Love," later known as "In the Summertime," and defined much of what would follow from Roger Miller. The song is up-tempo while the subject matter is about a man who has lost the love in his life, and features Roger's ad-libbed, bluesy scatting. The song made it to #14 on the country charts and was covered by pop crooner Andy Williams. "In the Summertime" also established Roger as a solo act. Less than a year later, Roger cracked the country top ten with "When Two Worlds Collide," a slow, weepy lament about what happens when people from different sides of life get together, and a title inspired by the sci-fi "B" film *When Two Worlds Collide* (1951), a favorite of Miller's. Those two songs were the highlight of Roger's RCA career as he was dropped in 1963 by the label after "Lock, Stock, and Teardrops" failed to gain any chart response, and Atkins reportedly tired of Miller's celebratory lifestyle.

Even though he had some success with his songwriting and performing, Miller did not get remotely wealthy, or even financially stable, from his work to that point. His next break came from television when his old friend Jimmy Dean, then guest hosting *The Tonight Show*, called Roger, whose walk-on performance of "I Walk the Line" with ad-libbed lyrics was an audience favorite. Appearances on other TV shows followed, and Roger decided he might have a better chance at a career in California than in Nashville. Smash Records entered the picture and picked up Roger in 1963. By January of 1964, Miller was ready for a session in which he cut fifteen songs with some of Nashville's top session musicians. Songs that came out of the session include 1964's million-selling Top Ten hit "Dang Me" and the catchy popular drinking song "Chug-a-Lug." However, the songs had not yet become hits, so Roger collected his

$1,500 for doing the session, moved to California, and landed upstairs from the eccentric country and pop songwriter and producer from Mannford, OK, Lee Hazlewood. While Roger was scrounging for gigs in California, "Dang Me" became a #1 country hit, staying on the chart for twenty-five weeks, and peaked on the pop charts at #7. The song changed his fortunes for good, and he became an in-demand performer on stage, TV, and in the recording studios. A few months later, "Chug-a-Lug" hit #3 on the country charts and #9 on the pop charts, and by fall Miller was back in the studio for Smash Records, recording "Do-Wacka-Do," a solid #15 hit on the country charts in 1964. Later that year, Miller recorded the song for which he has become most known, "King of the Road."

   Known by those close to Miller at the time as "the hobo song," "King of the Road" was released early in 1965 and in March hit #1 on the country charts where it remained for five weeks, made #4 on the pop charts, and by May had sold a million copies. In April 1965, Miller received five Grammy Awards for "Dang Me," to include Best Country Music Album, Single, Song, Vocal Performance, and, ironically, Best New Country and Western Artist. By the summer of 1965, Miller's career had reached its zenith, and he received his first royalty check for $168,000. Picked *Jukebox Magazine*'s Artist of the Year in 1965, Miller's crossover status inspired a number of mainstream press articles. *Life* magazine dubbed him a "cracker barrel philosopher," *Time* called him the "unhokey Okie," and in 1966 the *Saturday Evening Post* put him on the cover to represent a story chronicling the "Big Boom in Country Music." The 1966 Grammy Awards also showered Miller with awards for the previous year's "King of the Road," to include Best Country and Western Album, Single, Song, and three Best Vocal Performance Awards: Country, Contemporary and Rock and Roll. The Academy of Country Music also honored him with Songwriter, Man, and Single of the Year Awards for 1965.

Miller continued recording up-tempo songs mixing sad topics with humorous lyrics such as "My Uncle Used to Love Me but She Died," and tear-in-your beer ballads like "The Last Word in Lonesome is Me" and "Don't We All Have the Right to Be Wrong." Roger also became known for the occasional pop song of pure, if not naïve, happiness as in "Walkin' in the Sunshine." One of his most ironic songs was the postcard view of London in 1965's "England Swings." The song presented a complete opposite view of England from the one being represented by the British Invasion, and appealed to Anglo-Americans from whom the "old country" had become a comfortable stereotype.

By 1966, Roger was everywhere. Starting with his national fame in 1965, Roger made television appearances on the *Andy Williams Show*, *Dean Martin Show, Hollywood Palace with Bing Crosby, Tonight Show with Johnny Carson,* and *The Glen Campbell Goodtime Hour.* The Roger Miller Special aired in January of 1966, and NBC gave him his own TV show that featured many big names but was not renewed at the end of its thirteen-week run in 1966. On his last show, he blew up the train set used on the program so no one else would use it. Early in 1967, Roger had his last crossover hit as a writer, "Walkin' in the Sunshine;" and, later in the year he recorded, but did not write, the western soundtrack for the film *Waterhole #3.* Subsequently, as a recognizable country music voice, Miller proved his good ear for commercial tunes and turned to recording other people's songs, to include Bobby Russell's "Little Green Apples" in 1968, his last Top 40 crossover hit as an artist, and Kris Kristofferson's "Me and Bobby McGhee," a Top 20 country hit in 1969.

With his peak success years past, Miller recorded several country standards with honky-tonk arrangements in 1970 called *A Trip in the Country*. The album had no real impact, but "Don't We All Have the Right," which he had written in 1962 and included on the album, turned up on Ricky Van Shelton's first album *Wild-Eyed Dream* (1987), which indicated Roger's influence on young country singers. Mercury folded the Smash label in 1970, but not before Miller had one more minor chart single with "Hoppy's Song," about the death of singing cowboy Hopalong Cassidy, which Roger related to the end of an era in America. Columbia Records signed Miller after Smash folded, and Roger released *Dear Folks: Sorry I Haven't Written Lately*, which did not provide any hits.

In 1973, he wrote and sang songs for the Disney film *Robin Hood* and also appeared as the voice of Allan-A-Dale in the movie. That performance opened a new world of opportunities for his recognizable voiceovers and songs in productions aimed at children. He hosted and sang on *The Muppet Show* in the late 70s, and narrated several other youth-oriented features and specials throughout the remainder of his career. He also appeared in episodes of television programs such as *Love American Style*, *Daniel Boone* (as Johnny Appleseed), *Murder She Wrote*, and *Quincy* in which he played a singer with a substance abuse problem. Along with operating his King of the Road hotel chain, and making regular concert appearances, Roger continued recording moderate hits for Mercury and Elektra through the 1970s until 1982's *Old Friends*, on which he teamed up with old friends Willie Nelson and Ray Price.

With *Old Friends*, Roger made it back into the country Top Ten with the album's title track, written for his folks back in Oklahoma. Miller also enjoyed a significant resurgence of interest in his work when he was commissioned in 1984 to write songs for a Broadway musical adaptation of Mark Twain's *Adventures of Huckleberry Finn* called *Big River*. Broadway producer and long-time fan, Rocco Landesman, had seen Miller at a live appearance at New York City's Lone Star Café, and knew Roger would be perfect to write the music and songs of the musical that opened in 1985 and was huge hit. When actor John Goodman left for a film role, Roger played the part of Pap, based on Miller's uncle in Oklahoma, for a few months on Broadway and also on a national tour. Thanks to the show's success, Roger recorded a self-titled album for MCA in 1986, on which he sang several songs from the play, and *Big River* received seven Tony Awards, including Roger's for "Best Score." The extra attention induced the Academy of Country Music to give Roger their Pioneer Award for 1987, and *Big River* turned out to be the crowning achievement of his thirty-year career. The success of *Big River* led him to relax with his family until he was convinced by his manager and long-time friend, Stan Moress, to get back on the road, solo with guitar. The shows were met with enthusiastic response from critics and fans, but in the fall of 1991, Miller was diagnosed with lung cancer. His last performance was during CMA Week in Nashville; and, after a year of treatment, with one remission, he died in Nashville at the relatively young age of 56. In 1995, Miller was inducted posthumously into the Country Music Hall of Fame. His third and final wife, Mary Miller, a former singer with Kenny Rogers and the First Edition, and backup vocalist for Roger from the 1970s forward, said the induction "would have been his ultimate dream come true." He is survived by seven children: Alan, Rhonda, Shari, Dean, Shannon, Taylor, and Adam. Roger's posthumous fame has been significant.

Since 1992, at least forty-four albums have been released devoted fully or in part to Miller's recorded output, The Nashville Network aired a two-hour television special remembering Roger's life and music, featuring Reba McEntire, Willie Nelson, Trisha Yearwood and other country stars; and he received Grammy Hall of Fame Awards in 1997 and 1998. In 1999, his song "Husbands and Wives" was nominated as Song of the Year, and in one of the more significant "best of" lists produced in 2000, the Recording Industry of America and the National Endowment for the Arts listed "King of the Road" #84 on their combined "Songs of the Century" list. Roger's career sales included a platinum single (1,000,000 sold), six gold singles (500,000 sold each), and five gold albums (500,000 sold each). In 2003, CMT named "King of the Road" as one of the 100 Greatest Country Songs, placing it at #37 in the somewhat arbitrary list; and the musical *Big River* opened again on Broadway in November. Also in 2003, Roger's son Dean released an album on Universal South Records, the first single from which was called "The Gun Ain't Loaded." Finally, the people of Roger's hometown of Erick created the Roger Miller Museum Foundation in 2001, with the goal of building a museum to exhibit memorabilia from the life and career of yet another successful singing and songwriting Oklahoman. Miller certainly gained musical sense and his rural identity from the state, but his drive to accomplish his dreams, regardless of the sacrifice, produced lyrics that were at times melancholy and poignant, and other times celebratory and just downright silly, all of which parlayed into country and pop hits to which many people could relate. That was Roger Miller.

Live Music Venue in Erick

Currently, a kooky music streak still bubbles in the streets here at the Sand Hills Curiosity Shop, home to the Mediocre Music Makers, known for their humor, and musical ability with bluegrass and country music. The laid back, "out West" demeanor and hospitality of owners Annabelle and Harley Russell have made the spot a favorite for tour buses traveling through. Located downtown on Sheb Wooley Street. For more information call (580) 526-3738.

Annual Music Events

Oklahoma vs. Texas Bar-B-Q Competition, musical entertainment, May, (580) 526-3837.
Annual Honey Festival, live music, second weekend of Nov.

For More Information About Erick

Erick Chamber of Commerce, 118 Roger Miller Boulevard (580) 526-3505 or www.rogermiller.com.

Texola

Established in 1902 as a border town at the junction of Oklahoma and Texas for the Rock Island Line.

2000 Population: At 47, Texola is the smallest town on Oklahoma Historic Route 66, but to say the town is dwindling is not accurate, as the population is up from 45 in 1990.

Live Music Venues

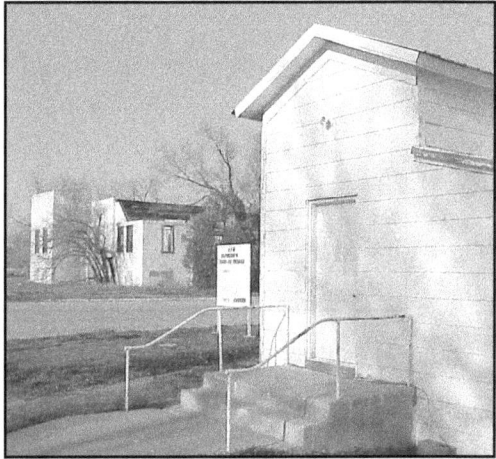

With two churches and two taverns in Texola, weekend nights or Sunday mornings are the best bet for music and spiritual sustenance before leaving, or just getting into, Oklahoma.

Water Hole #2 is just inside the Oklahoma border in Texola.

For More Information

Double D Fuel, Rest Stop, and Campground, I-40 (Exit 1), (580) 526-3967 or try the Erick Chamber of Commerce.

In Memory

Claude "Fiddler" Williams (2/22/1908 - 4/27/2004)
Barney Kessel (10/17/1923 - 5/6/2004)
Verbie "Flash" Terry (6/17/1934 - 3/18/2004)

Red Dirt Music (Revised)

Red Dirt Music (Revised)

from the first edition of the *Oklahoma Music Guide* (2003)

With Jimmy LaFave, Tom Skinner, Bob Childers, The Great Divide, Red Dirt Rangers, Cross Canadian Ragweed, Jason Boland and the Stragglers, and a host of other rootsy singer songwriters and groups leading the way, the multi-influenced music known as red dirt music is varying degrees of blues, country, Tin Pan Alley, rock and roll, folk, and cowboy songs, often delivered with lyrically sardonic humor that is often dry as the red earth around north central Oklahoma, to include Bristow, Oklahoma City, Enid, and especially Stillwater where its primary musicians met, usually as college students at Oklahoma State University. When humor is not the object of the song's lyrically focused intent, subtle and melancholy appraisals of rural and small town society's decay fill the verses of red dirt music, and, occasionally, a song about love lost or gained creeps or weeps its way into the mix. A great example of the music and its touchstones can be found on *Music from the All-American Highway: The Songs of Route 66.* The Red Dirt Rangers, Jimmy LaFave, Kevin Welch all offer takes on what Welch calls the "Willy Rogers Highway."

The first Oklahoman to hint at the "genre" is Kiowa-Comanche-Muscogee guitarist Jesse Ed Davis (right), whose "Red Dirt Boogie, Brother," a funky, self-defining tune about "plain old rock and roll," appeared on his 1972 album Ululu (Atco). Close behind in name, if not definition, is Steve Ripley whose early 1970s band, Moses, recorded for Ripley's independent Red Dirt Records. Liner notes by Mike

Dougan on the band's self-titled debut in 1974 explain Red Dirt is a record label and "also the color of the earth surrounding Enid and nearby Stillwater, Moses' home base. More important, Red Dirt is a hue of funk, a shade of sound, a basic spirit embodied in Moses' music."

While the genre's anthem is Jimmy LaFave's "Red Dirt Roads at Night," and LaFave recorded his first album in Stillwater in 1978, the first artist to emerge on a national scale from the Stillwater scene was Garth Brooks who began singing at Willie's Saloon on Washington Street in 1985. After a failed attempt that year at breaking through Nashville's long established musical hierarchy, Brooks returned to Stillwater and started a group called Santa Fe in 1986. Filling out Santa Fe were Tom Skinner, roundly considered along with Bob Childers as one of red dirt music's early shapers, as well as Tom's brothers Mike and Craig, on fiddle and guitar respectively, and other Stillwater musicians such as Matt O'Melia (drums), Dale Pierce (steel guitar and dobro), and Jed Lindsey (guitar). A particularly good take on the early Stillwater scene that produced Santa Fe can be gleaned from drummer O'Melia's book about those years, Garth Brooks: The Road Out of Santa Fe (University of Oklahoma Press, 1997). After graduating from OSU with a degree in marketing, Garth again headed for Nashville. There, he connected with Bob Childers who introduced the one-time OSU javelin thrower to the manager who ignited Brooks' star in the country music firmament.

Bob Childers(left) was born in West Virginia, studied music at the University of California-Berkeley, and began traveling the country in 1972 when he arrived in Stillwater and discovered Chuck Dunlap, a local Stillwater-based singer songwriter who still reigns as the elder statesman of the movement. Childers decided to stay in Stillwater and played locally until 1978 when he met Jimmy LaFave. With LaFave's assistance, Bob recorded his first album, *I Ain't No Jukebox* (1979). Childers' second album, 1982's *Singing Trees, Dancing Waters*, gained him enough critical attention for a White House gig in Washington, D.C., and enough confidence to move to Nashville in 1986, followed closely by Tom Skinner and Garth.

Childers released two albums in 1986, *Four Horsemen*, and the all-instrumental *King David's Lament.* Nashville's "smooth" requirements ultimately alienated Childers, and the songwriter moved to Austin where he recorded *Circles Toward the Sun* (1990) that produced a couple of minor regional hits, "Restless Spirits" and "Mexican Mornings." Finally coming full circle, Childers moved back to Stillwater in 1996 and recorded an album that received considerable attention in Europe, *Nothin' More Natural* (Binky Records). Bob's 1999 CD, *Hat Trick*, featured songs co-written by Mike McClure (The Great Divide), Brad Piccolo (Red Dirt Rangers), and Garth Brooks. Bob also added two tracks to The Great Divide and Friends 1999 gospel album, *Dirt and Spirit*. In 2000, Binky Records released Childers' *La Vita e Bella – Outtakes, Demos and Jams 1980 – 1988*. According to the Binky Records website, Bob's future music industry plans were on hold in 2003 while he "was concentrating on the education of his children." Nonetheless, younger red dirt musicians continue recording his songs, such as the Red Dirt Rangers (pictured at right),

Cross Canadian Ragweed, Jason Boland and the Stragglers (right), and Stoney LaRue who included Childers' "Dance with the Gypsies" on LaRue's 2002 CD, *Downtown* (Lone Star Music). As much as any musician, Childers defines the genre, often known by fans as a "Dylan of the dust," or simply, "the Godfather."

Although Tom Skinner was born in San Francisco, he and his two musically inclined brothers, Mike and Craig, grew up in the Route 66 town of Bristow about thirty miles southwest of Tulsa. Skinner moved to Stillwater in 1972 where a short attempt at Oklahoma State University bore few fruits other than Skinner's first guitar chords. After a stint in the Air Force where he played in his first bands, Tom returned to Oklahoma in 1978 and re-enrolled at Oklahoma State. Soon, his brothers followed and they soon began performing around town as The Skinner Brothers Band, most notably at Willie's Saloon where Garth Brooks also frequented the open microphone nights. Garth hooked up with the brothers who eventually became the nucleus of his first group, Santa Fe, where the evolving red dirt sound began to take solid commercial shape. Skinner moved to Nashville for a short time in the late 1980s, but returned to Oklahoma for his young son's sake, and ultimately migrated to Louisiana where he began recording for Binky Records, to include *Times Have Changed* (1996), and *Acoustic Skinner* (1998). Skinner continues to perform in Oklahoma at venues such as the Blue Door in Oklahoma City, itself a primary outlet for the sound, and can be seen regularly at any number of festivals, showcases, and other events throughout the state.

Along with Bob Childers' albums, Binky has also released two compact discs by Greg Jacobs, the Choctaw, Oklahoma native who found his way to Stillwater in the 1970s for college, and turned into another singer-songwriter now associated with the red dirt sound. After rambling through Kentucky and then taking a shot at the Nashville scene that did not take to his highly personal songs, Jacobs returned to Oklahoma. Working as an opening act for Kevin Welch and Jimmy LaFave, Jacobs recorded two independent albums, *Looking at the Moon* (1994), and *Reclining with Age* (1996) Currently a high school history teacher in Checotah, Jacobs' albums, *South of Muskogee Town* (1997) and *Look at Love* (1999), are chock full of stories about Oklahoma's hard rural history in the 20th century - "A Little Rain Will Do," and "Okie Wind," as well as seldom-told stories like that of Muscogee (Creek) patriot Chitto Harjo in "South of Muskogee Town," a song about the Green Corn Rebellion of 1918. His 2001 release that recycled an earlier album title, *Reclining with Age* (Binky), continued Jacobs' themes and storytelling style of his earlier releases.

Young bands and singer-songwriters have played local talent nights and open microphones in Stillwater for as long as college students have been drinking beer in the north central Oklahoma town, but a unique environment opened in May of 1979 when John Cooper (Red Dirt Rangers) and recreation specialist major Danny Pierce moved into a rural six-bedroom farmhouse on 149 acres for a hundred bucks a month. Only a few miles west of Stillwater, "The Farm" quickly gained a reputation as a communal jam space, party center, and flophouse for local musicians and college students throughout the 1980s and 1990s. Roughly sixty roommates moved through The Farm during its twenty-year existence, and although the Red Dirt Rangers' Brad Piccolo didn't live there, he was a constant presence and credits his inspiration for seeking a music career to seeing Jimmy LaFave singing a Bob Dylan song on the front porch one night. Also present at various times were Bob Childers, Tom Skinner, Greg Jacobs, and Garth, all of whom headed out to The Farm when Stillwater's bars closed and musicians still had the desire to jam. Texas singer-songwriter Robert Earl Keen stopped by at one time or another where bonfires were set and musicians played until dawn, as did Brandon Jenkins, Mark Lyons, Curt Nielsen, and Chuck Dunlap. Dunlap recorded a 1980 album called *Daze Gone By* (Snowbound), featuring Kevin Welch on guitar, and sporting a jazzy, folk feel with pedal steel, bongos, saxophone, banjo, and plenty of harmony vocals.

In the last year or two of The Farm's existence, before a Methodist church bought the property in 1999, relative newcomers to Stillwater, Cody Canada of Cross Canadian Ragweed, Mike McClure of the Great Divide, and Jason Boland emerged on the scene. Boland had one of the Stragglers' first promo pictures taken on the porch of The Farm, and images of the now legendary homestead have been forever preserved on Mike McClure's website (www.mikemcclure.com). Other bands that played in the garage, the front room, the basement, or the fields throughout the 1990s included the Cimarron Swingsters, the Red Valley Barnstormers, the Flat Mountain Boys, and the Medicine Show, whose 1994 album, *Medicine Show Live at the Tower Theater*, stirs up great jam clouds of red dirt music, as does their 1997 release, *Midnight Ramble,* recorded live in Fayetville, Arkansas.

  While the Delicious Militia did not play at The Farm, their lyrically twisted, if not gifted, 1998 country rock album, *What Ever Happened to the Banjo Girl* (Hog Frost), featured several Stillwater college students, to include OSU Rhodes Scholar and Hydro, Oklahoma native Blaine Greteman, who went on to be the London entertainment editor for *Time* Magazine, and, as of 2003, was a Ph.D. candidate at the University of California at Berkeley. Other local Stillwater artists who have close connections to the scene include Mitch Cason, Beverly Mayes, and DaddyO's Music owner, songwriter and guitarist, Mike Shannon (b. Tulsa, 1953). Also, Monica Taylor and Patrick Williams, both Cherokee Nation citizens better known as The Farm Couple, have been performing together since 1996 when they debuted at the Winfield Bluegrass Festival. Monica was living at The Farm at that time, and Patrick was living near Grove, Oklahoma. Their independent CD, *Songs from the Kitchen Table*, was recorded in "one take per song" in a studio overlooking a lake in Eureka Springs, Arkansas, and features songs about ramblers, Civil War veterans, and other down-and-outers.

  Additional musicians who have been placed in the red dirt genre (whether they like it or not) include Tulsa-based Larry Spears, whose CD, *Reflection in the Wishing Well*, featuring songs about Woody Guthrie, Jesus, and better times that have passed. Tom Skinner also adds bass and vocals to the album. The Burtschi Brothers from Norman have also been allied with the sound. The Brothers' band includes Travis Linville (guitar) Mike Phenix (bass), Kevin Webb (guitars), and Chris Foreman (drums). Exhibiting the back-and-forth-from-Oklahoma-to-Texas-nature of red dirt groups, The Burtschi Brothers' debut album, *Uncertain Texas*, was recorded in Linville's Norman bedroom, and after a little success, the group recorded CD number two in Austin, Texas. Next, their most recent effort was recorded live in Tahlequah and exhibits their extended jams where "Jimi Hendrix meets Willie Nelson in outer space."

Another Oklahoma native musician with red dirt tendencies, Brandon Jenkins (b. June 7, 1969, Tulsa), has made his home in Austin after growing up in Tulsa. Jenkins (right) attended Oklahoma State where he graduated with a B.A. in Sociology, tried out Nashville for a while after he had signed with a label in Alabama that tried to market him as a country act, and then returned to Tulsa before heading south across the border to Austin's intensely music friendly environment. Jenkins' 1998 CD, *Faded*, brands his style as "Western Soul, a hybrid of country, blues, and rock-n-roll," which allies it closely with basic tenets of red dirt music. A song Jenkins wrote in Stillwater, "Feet Don't Touch the Ground," was included on a Pete Anderson produced compilation of America's best unsigned artists outside of Nashville called *Country West of Nashville* (2001). In 2003, Jenkins released his next project, *Unmended*, and continued touring throughout Texas and Oklahoma in 2004.

Two of the latest arrivals on the red dirt scene are Amanda Cunningham (b. 1978) and Stoney LaRue and the Organic Boogie Band. Cunningham's independent CD, *Gypsy's Daughter*, mines the red dirt vein well enough to have earned her the *Oklahoma Gazette*'s 2003 Woody Award for Best Singer/Songwriter in Oklahoma. Larue, who is originally from Texas but has spent much of his time in Oklahoma since his teens, guides the Organic Boogie Band through twelve songs on their debut CD, *Downtown.* The album is drenched in red dirt influences, with two songs co-written by LaRue and Jason Boland, and covers of songs by Brandon Jenkins, Bob Childers, and Mike McClure.

A final figure of note is multi-instrumentalist, music teacher, studio artist, and recording engineer Jeffrey Gray Parker who lived in Stillwater from 1989 to 1998. With two albums under his studio alter ego, Coyote Zen, influenced not only by the red dirt sound and his own American Indian (Cherokee) background, *Blood of Many Nations* (1997) and *Medicine Dog* (2002) also fuse multiple world music elements into unique releases that transcend the red dirt genre. As a performer, Parker has traveled widely and played with a myriad of nationally recognized artists (Buck Owens, Kevin Welch, Ricochet, Rita Coolidge, Alice Cooper, Brewer and Shipley, Kevin Welch, et al.), and has had his music used in various film and television projects, as well as radio and television commercials.

Aside from Jeffrey Parker's individual releases, his Cimarron Sound Lab in Stillwater was the site for the recording of *Red Dirt Sampler*, *Volume 1: A Stillwater Songwriters' Collective*. The album is a primer for red dirt music fans. Songs by all the first generation of the sound's luminaries, Tom Skinner, Brad James (lead guitarist for the Organic Boogie Band), Mike McClure, Greg Jacobs, Bob Childers are on the CD, as well as songs co-written by Parker with Skinner and Bob Kline.

While DaddyO's is still on Main Street, and two of the Red Dirt Rangers live in rural areas east of Stillwater near the small town of Glencoe, by 2004 many of the musicians who created the scene moved on to Tulsa, Oklahoma City, Austin, Nashville, or back to the small Oklahoma towns they had left behind for college. Perhaps even the term itself has left the area.

In the spring of 2003, country pop act Brooks & Dunn, featuring Ronnie Dunn, who has deep Tulsa ties, released *Red Dirt Road* (ARISTA), featuring a #1 country single by the same name that is a rowdy tribute to the lessons of rural life learned out on the dusty crimson pathways of the country. In 2004, many of the artists mentioned here were featured on a collection of songs inspired by Route 66, *Songs of the Mother Road* (Yellow Dog Records).

Contemporarily, red dirt music may often only be a tag placed on musicians from the Stillwater area (and now much of central Oklahoma right through which Route 66 passes) who write their own songs and play in traditional American music veins. Even though some of its progenitors have wearied of the label, the category is useful for describing music that is at times one person with a guitar and a story to tell, and at other times a gutsy jam band freak-out not afraid of a little twang; all of which draws inspiration from Woody Guthrie's lyrical abilities, Bob Wills' wide open approach to popular music, and Will Rogers' plain-spoken humor to create a sound and story unique to Oklahoma.

www.reddirtmusic.com
www.bobchilders.com
www.organicboogieband.com
http://members.aol.com/straycatm/tomskinner.htm
www.binkyrecords.com
www.brandonjenkins.net
www.bluedoorokc.com
www.amandasmusic.com
www.coyotezen.com

Nostalgic Radio Stations Audible on Route 66 from Chicago to Los Angeles

Chicago, Illinois
WXCD-FM, 94.7 – Oldies
WLUP-FM, 97.9 – Classic Rock
WKSC-FM, 103.5 – Oldies
WJMK-FM, 104.3 – Oldies

Springfield, Illinois
WQQL-FM, 101.9 – Oldies

Springfield, Missouri
KTOZ-AM, 1060 – Big Band, Nostalgia
KXUS-FM, 97.3 – Classic Rock
KWTO-FM, 98.7 – Classic Rock

St. Louis, Missouri
WEW-AM, 770 – Big Band, Oldies
KIHT- FM, 96.3 – Classic Rock
KLOU-FM, 103.3 – Oldies

Tulsa, Oklahoma
KRMG-AM, 740 – Weather Information – Listen for "ping" to indicate severe weather
KGTO-AM, 1050 – 6am to Sunset, Urban Classics
KFAQ-AM, 1170 – Weather Information, News Talk
KOTV-FM, 87.7 – CBS Affiliate KOTV-TV audio
KRSC-FM, 91.3 – 6 a.m. to 10 p.m. College Radio
KBEZ-FM, 92.9 – Adult Pop/ Big Band Saturday Nights
KWEN-FM, 95.5 – Contemporary Country and Classics
KMOD FM, 97.5 – Classic Rock, Modern Rock
KVOO-FM, 98.5 – Classic Country
KJJR-FM, 103.3 – Classic Rock
KMYZ-FM, 104.5 – Modern Rock/Classic Alternative Hits
KOOL-FM, 106.1 – Oldies

Oklahoma City, Oklahoma
WKY-AM, 930 – Weather Information
KTOK-AM, 1000 – News, Talk, Weather Information
KVSP-AM, 1140 – Urban Contemporary and Classics
KOMA-FM, 92.5 – Oldies
KATT-FM, 100.5 – Contemporary and Classic Rock
KTST-FM, 101.9 – Contemporary and Classic Country
KSYY-FM, 105.3 – Modern Rock and Alternative Classics
KRXO-FM, 107.7 – Classic Rock

Amarillo, Texas
KBZD-FM, 99.7 – Blues
KPUR-FM, 107 – Oldies

Tucumcari, New Mexico
KTNM-AM, 1400 – Contemporary Country and Classics

Albuquerque, New Mexico
KIVA-AM, 1580 – Oldies
KPEK-FM, 100.3 – Oldies

Gallup, New Mexico
KGAK-AM, 1330 – American Indian Music
KTHR-AM, 1230 – Contemporary and Classic Country
KXXI-FM, 93.7 – Classic Rock

Flagstaff, Arizona
KMGN-FM, 93.9 – Classic Rock

Barstow, California
KXXZ-FM, 95.9 – Classic Rock

San Bernadino, California
KOLA-FM, 99.9 – Oldies

Los Angeles, California
KLAC-AM, 570 – Oldies
KCBS-FM, 93.1 – Classic Rock, Adult Contemporary
KKBT-FM, 100.3 – Oldies, Adult Contemporary

Additional Oklahoma Route 66 Music and History Resources

Carney, George O. and Hugh W. Foley, Jr. *Oklahoma Music Guide*. Stillwater: New Forums Press, 2003.

Carney, George O., ed. *Sounds of People and Places: A Geography of American Music from Country to Classical and Blues to Bop*. 4th edition. Oxford: Rowman and Littlefield, 2003.

Morris, John W., Charles R. Goins, and Edwin C. McReynolds. *Historical Atlas of Oklahoma*. University of Oklahoma Press, 1987.

Official Oklahoma Route 66 Association Trip Guide, 2003-2004. Oklahoma City: www.oklahomaroute66.com.

Oklahoma Almanac: 2003-2004. 49th ed. (Revised) Oklahoma City: Oklahoma Department of Libraries, 2003.

Roads of Oklahoma. Fredericksburg, TX: Shearer Publishing, 1997.

Ross, Jim. *Oklahoma Route 66*. Ghost Town Press, 2001.

Ruth, Kent. *Oklahoma Travel Handbook*. University of Oklahoma Press, 1985 (3rd printing).

Shirk, George H., and Muriel H. Wright. *Oklahoma Place Names*. University of Oklahoma Press, 1987.

Wright, Muriel, H. *A Guide to the Indian Tribes of Oklahoma*. Norman: University of Oklahoma Press, 1986.

Photo and Image Credits

The authors credit the following artists, photographers, record labels, and publicity services for providing images for this guide. If any information included in these credits is incorrect, or if an image's copyright has been improperly transferred to its placement in this text, please contact the authors for a timely resolution and/or correction for future editions of the *Oklahoma Route 66 Music Guide*. Send comments, concerns, or additional images to authors@oklahomamusicguide.com or New Forums Press, 1018 South Lewis Street, Stillwater, Oklahoma, 74074, U.S.A.

All images not otherwise credited were made by Hugh Foley or are part of the Hugh Foley collection.

Rascal Flatts image courtesy Universal Music and Video Distribution; Jimmie Rivers image courtesy Joaquin Records from Jimmie Rivers and the Cherokees, *Brisbane Bop Western Swing 1961-64* (JR2501); Louis Ballard photo by Abe Eilot courtesy of Louis Ballard; Cherokee fiddler Sam O'Fields courtesy of Cara Cowan; Cherokee National Holiday program cover courtesy Cherokee Nation of Oklahoma; Steve Gaines cover image with Cassie Gaines from *I Know a Little Live* courtesy Teresa Gaines Rapp; Ace Moreland album cover *Give It To Get It* (IHR 9438) photo by Peter M. Everett courtesy icehouse and King Snake Records; Patti Page image from *Patti Page's Golden Hits* (MG 20495) courtesy of Mercury Records; Muscogee (Creek) traditional images courtesy Tallahassee (Wvkokye) Ceremonial Grounds; Image of Leon Russell courtesy MCA Records; GAP Band image courtesy Universal Music and Video Distribution;

Norma Jean image courtesy of Norma Jean; Mikaila image courtesy of Universal Music and Video Distribution; University of Central Oklahoma performance image courtesy of University of Central Oklahoma Department of Theatre Arts; Byron Berline image courtesy Byron Berline; Cross Canadian Ragweed image courtesy Universal Music and Video Distribution; The John Simpson Orchestra courtesy of www.czechhall.com; Sam Rivers photo by Steve Salmieri courtesy of Tomato Records; Caddo Drum group courtesy of the Caddo Nation; Kiowa Gourd Clan images with permission of the Kiowa Gourd Clan; Eldon Shamblin courtesy of Don Tolle; Jimmy Webb image courtesy of Jimmy Webb; Bob Childers courtesy Bob Childers; Brandon Jenkins image courtesy of Brandon Jenkins; Jesse Ed Davis image courtesy of Jack Dunham; Jason Boland image courtesy of Brandy Reed of RPR Marketing and Public Relations, Nashville.

Acknowledgements

The authors would like to thank the following individuals and organizations for assisting us in completing this guide:

Doug and Gayla Dollar for suggesting the idea for a guide to the music of Route 66 in Oklahoma, and then publishing the book; the Rogers State University Department of Communications and Fine Arts for continued support and friendship; Michael Wallis for his monumental leadership in Route 66 scholarship and interpretations of the road's cultural significance; Jim Ross for his important maps of Oklahoma's Route 66 path; Pat Smith at the Oklahoma Route 66 Museum for encouraging this work; Mary Jane Warde and Rodger Harris at the Oklahoma Historical Society; the librarians at Rogers State University; Michael P. Larson, Cartography Services, Oklahoma State University, for creating the maps of Route 66 for this guide; Jeana and Emily Dial-Driver for editing the manuscript under pressure and on short notice; the Oklahoma Route 66 Association for their encouragement and hospitality at the 2004 International Route 66 Festival in Tulsa; Nokose and Geri Foley for enduring yet another book project by Hugh; and the many people we have met along the old road that have inspired us to continue celebrating this important icon of Americana.

Authors

Dr. George O. Carney (right), Regents Professor of Geography at Oklahoma State University in Stillwater, has authored three books on American music, including *Fast Food, Stock Cars, and Rock 'n' Roll* (1995), *Baseball, Barns, and Bluegrass* (1998), and *The Sounds of People and Places* (2002). In addition, he has contributed more than 50 scholarly articles and book chapters on American music to such publications as *Popular Music and Society*, *Country Music Annual*, *Journal of Geography*, *Journal of Cultural Geography*, *The Canadian Geographer*, and *GeoJournal*. He has published two major monographs chronicling Oklahoma music—*A Biographical Dictionary of Oklahoma Jazz Artists* (1992) and *Oklahoma Women in American Music* (1999). Carney is also a member of the Friends of Oklahoma Music Board of Directors and the Governor's Oklahoma Music Hall of Fame Board. Carney and Hugh Foley co-authored *Oklahoma Music Guide: Biographies, Big Hits, and Annual Events* in 2003. Dr. Carney resides in Stillwater with his wife, Janie.

An assistant professor of communications and fine arts at Rogers State University in Claremore, Dr. Hugh W. Foley, Jr. has contributed scholarly articles, book chapters, and encyclopedia entries on American Indian music, rock, jazz, blues, and country music to *The Oklahoma Encyclopedia of the Humanities* (2007), *The Sound of People and Places* (2003), *The New York Encyclopedia of the Humanities* (2002), *The Guide to United States Popular Culture* (2001), and *Living Blues* (1998). He is a charter member of the Friends of Oklahoma Music (FOM) Board of Directors, having served as vice-president as well as chair of the Oklahoma Music Hall of Fame induction selection committee. Foley has also been actively involved in radio since 1977, during which time he has worked as a disc-jockey, program director, music director, and announcer at stations in Oklahoma, Atlanta, GA, New York City, Berkeley, CA, Germany, and Japan. Currently, he is the music director for 1600, KUSH AM, an independent Americana station in Cushing, Oklahoma, as well as serving as the faculty music consultant at 91.3, KRSC-FM, the student radio station at Rogers State University. He lives in Stillwater with his wife, Geri, and their son, Nokose.

Foley and Carney

Notes

Notes

Win a FREE Copy
of
The Oklahoma Music Guide

Just identify the following four musical images visible from the road along Oklahoma Historic Route 66. Send in your answers (or any other comments) to the *Oklahoma Route 66 Music Guide*, Box 876, Stillwater, Oklahoma, U.S.A. 74076, or authors@oklahomamusicguide.com. If you are correct, we will send you a free copy of the 688-page reference work, *Oklahoma Music Guide: Biographies, Big Hits, and Annual Events,* that further explores the music, musicians, tribes, songs and related Oklahoma music history briefly introduced in this book.

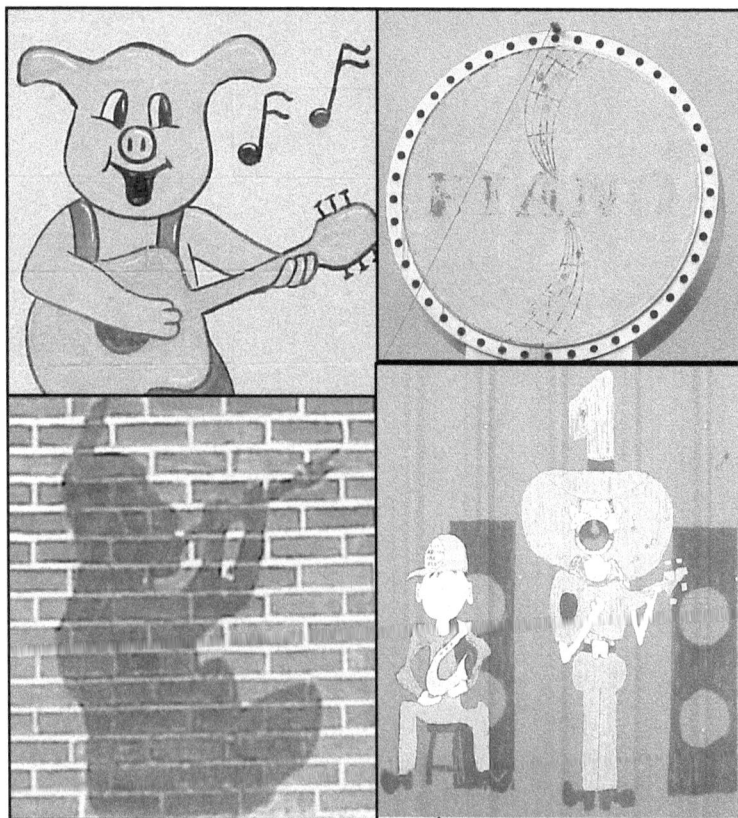

Special Titles from New Forums Press
call 1-800-606-3766 or go to www.newforums.com to order!

Oklahoma Cowboy Cartoons
-by Daryl Talbot

Award-winning cartoonist Daryl Talbot returns with this collection of cartoons depicting the funny side of modern cowboyin'. If you've ever owned a horse or worked on a ranch (or wished you did), you'll get a kick out of this lighthearted look at ranchin' and ropin'.

1999 (ISBN: 1-58107-014-4; 64 pages, 5 1/2 x 8 1/2, soft cover) $ 7.95

Between Me & You & the Gatepost — Rural Expressions of Oklahoma
(2nd, enlarged edition)

-by Jim Etter, illustrated by Daryl Talbot

A new and bigger edition of this popular collection of homegrown expressions and euphemisms that have distinguished the speech of Oklahoma folks for a coon's age and may do so 'til the cows come home. Take the bull by the horns and buy this book, and you'll be grinnin' like a possum eatin' persimmons!

1999 (ISBN: 1-58107-015-2; 44 pages, 5 1/2 x 8 1/2, soft cover) $ 7.95

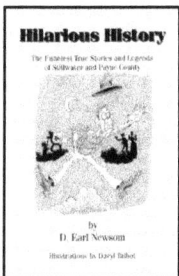

Hilarious History: The Funniest True Stories and Legends of Stillwater and Payne County
-by D. Earl Newsom

A collection of many true stories of the early days of Stillwater and Payne County that in retrospect are hilarious, although they often involved bitter controversies at the time: adultery, fist-fighting attorneys, bootlegging preachers, and preachers' bitter debates (and fist fights). Taken from contemporary newspaper accounts.

1999 (ISBN: 1-58107-016-0; 60 pages, 5 1/2 x 8 1/2, soft cover) $ 7.95

The Cherokee Strip—Its History & Grand Opening
–by D. Earl Newsom

The opening of the Cherokee Outlet, popularly known as the Cherokee Strip, on September 16, 1893, was one of the great spectacles of American history. Relive the excitement in this outstanding volume. Includes a history of the Cherokee Nation; the towns of Alma, Blackwell, Enid, Newkirk, Perry, Ponca City, and Woodward, along with the 101 Ranch. Illustrated with 160 historical photographs.

1992 (ISBN: 0-913507-27-X; 209 pages, 6 x 9 inch, soft cover)   **$13.95**

Ragged Edges: Unusual Rag-Time Compositions
–by John Wilson

Here is a true delight for those interested in early Oklahoma history. Ragtime was the music of the period of the land-run and early statehood , the music that inspired, entertained, and delighted the pioneer forefathers of Oklahoma! You will be tapping your feet to Professor Wilson's skillful rendering of Eli Green's Cake Walk, Mandy's Ragtime Waltz, The Watermelon Trust Slow Drag, and others. And, those who play the piano will certainly enjoy trying their fingers at these invigorating tunes. **Includes audio cassette.**

1998 (ISBN: 0-913507-98-0; 122 pages, 8 1/2 x 11, soft cover, lay-flat binding)   **$25.00**

A Distant Flame: *The Inspiring Story of Jack VanBebber's Quest for a World Olympic Title*
–by Jack VanBebber as told to Julia VanBebber

The autobiography of a sickly and partially handicapped Oklahoma boy who developed his abilities to become an NCAA champion wrestler at Oklahoma A&M, win a 1932 Olympic Gold Medal, and eventually be known as one of the ten greatest amateur wrestlers of all times. A must for young readers and sports fans.

1992 (ISBN: 0-913507-26-1; 192 pages , 5 1/2 x 8 1/2, soft cover)   **$13.95**

www.ingramcontent.com/pod-product-compliance
Lightning Source LLC
Chambersburg PA
CBHW051959090426
42741CB00008B/1463